T0358344

Cambridge Elements ☰

Elements in Ancient and Pre-modern Economies
edited by
Kenneth G. Hirth
The Pennsylvania State University
Timothy Earle
Northwestern University
Emily J. Kate
The University of Vienna

NORDIC BRONZE AGE ECONOMIES

Christian Horn
University of Gothenburg

Knut Ivar Austvoll
University of Oslo

Johan Ling
University of Gothenburg

Magnus Artursson
University of Gothenburg

CAMBRIDGE
UNIVERSITY PRESS

Shaftesbury Road, Cambridge CB2 8EA, United Kingdom

One Liberty Plaza, 20th Floor, New York, NY 10006, USA

477 Williamstown Road, Port Melbourne, VIC 3207, Australia

314–321, 3rd Floor, Plot 3, Splendor Forum, Jasola District Centre,
New Delhi – 110025, India

103 Penang Road, #05–06/07, Visioncrest Commercial, Singapore 238467

Cambridge University Press is part of Cambridge University Press & Assessment,
a department of the University of Cambridge.

We share the University's mission to contribute to society through the pursuit of
education, learning and research at the highest international levels of excellence.

www.cambridge.org
Information on this title: www.cambridge.org/9781009475839

DOI: 10.1017/9781009421416

First published 2024

A catalogue record for this publication is available from the British Library

ISBN 978-1-009-47583-9 Hardback
ISBN 978-1-009-42142-3 Paperback
ISSN 2754-2955 (online)
ISSN 2754-2947 (print)

Cambridge University Press & Assessment has no responsibility for the persistence
or accuracy of URLs for external or third-party internet websites referred to in this
publication and does not guarantee that any content on such websites is, or will
remain, accurate or appropriate.

Nordic Bronze Age Economies

Elements in Ancient and Pre-modern Economies

DOI: 10.1017/9781009421416
First published online: December 2024

Christian Horn
University of Gothenburg

Knut Ivar Austvoll
University of Oslo

Johan Ling
University of Gothenburg

Magnus Artursson
University of Gothenburg

Author for correspondence: Christian Horn, christian.horn@gu.se

Abstract: In this Element, we provide a multiscalar synthesis of Nordic Bronze Age economies (1800/1700–500 BCE) that is organized around six sections: an introduction to the Nordic Bronze Age, macroeconomic perspectives, defining local communities, economic interaction, conflict and alliances, political formations, and encountering Europe. Despite a unifying material culture, the Bronze Age of Scandinavia was complex and multilayered with constantly shifting and changing networks of competitors and partners. The social structure in this highly mobile and dynamic macro-regional setting was affected by subsistence economies based on agropastoralism, maritime sectors, the production of elaborate metal wealth, trade in a wide range of goods, as well as raiding and warfare. For this reason, the focus of this Element is on the integration and interaction of subsistence and political economies in a comparative analysis between different local constellations within the macroeconomic setting of prehistoric Europe. This title is also available as open access on Cambridge Core.

Keywords: Nordic Bronze Age, economy, Southern Scandinavia, local communities, interaction

ISBNs: 9781009475839 (HB), 9781009421423 (PB), 9781009421416 (OC)
ISSNs: 2754-2955 (online), 2754-2947 (print)

Contents

1 The Nordic Bronze Age

This Element describes the regional economic underpinnings of the social and political development of the Nordic Bronze Age (NordicBA). This encompasses the modern countries of Denmark, Sweden, Norway, the southwestern coast of Finland, and the northernmost part of Germany (Figure 1). Within this cultural sphere extending well over 565,000 km² was one of the most diverse regions in Europe in terms of landscape and ecological zones. Yet it also formed a relatively homogeneous cultural expression in socioeconomic organization and material culture including a distinct Nordic metalwork style, rock art, building, and burial traditions.

This Element aims to introduce the economic relationships of NordicBA societies and to unravel their complexity. For this, we outline the interlocking systems of domestic and political economies. Local communities had the same needs for survival and social reproduction but faced different challenges through their geographical and environmental setting. To highlight this, we aim to detail land-based and sea-based sectors of production as well as social formations split into cooperative and coercive societies. To fulfill their needs, these societies engaged in economic exchange at different scales which we introduce in the sections of this Element. Scales include long-distance interaction with other cultural groups in Europe all the way down to local interactions between neighboring farmsteads. To provide a holistic overview of the various modes such economic interactions could take, we will consider trade and alliance formation, but also violent actions such as raiding and slave-taking. To frame the tension between the need for such interaction and the attempt of the NordicBA communities to be as self-sufficient as possible, we will introduce the overarching concept of the maritime mode of production (MMP) to help understand how complexity emerged at relatively low population densities. Ultimately, we hope to provide a readable and easy-to-use account that helps to understand the economies of the NordicBA as phenomena with several dimensions and scales, and different objectives, without smoothing over tensions and conflicting aspects.

The emergence of the NordicBA was a long process with cycles of technological innovations, social changes, and significant micro-regional differences. At the beginning of the Neolithic (c. 4000 BCE), cereal cultivation and animal husbandry were first introduced in southern Scandinavia by groups of the Funnelbeaker culture (FBC) (e.g., Gron et al., 2015; Sørensen and Karg, 2014). Although evidence of early cereal cultivation exists in Middle Sweden and South Norway in the Early and Middle Neolithic, a sedentary economy with cereal cultivation takes first

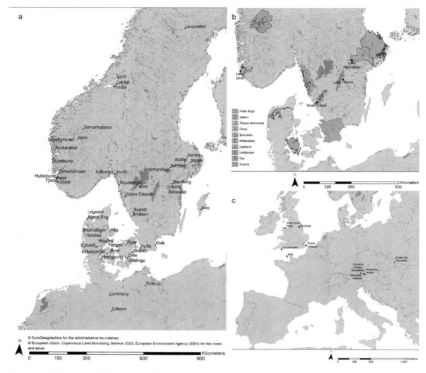

Figure 1 Maps of (a) sites, (b) regions, lakes, and rivers, and (c) European sites and regions mentioned in the text (produced by Ashely Green)

hold in the Late Neolithic (LN) (c. 2350 BCE) in these areas (e.g., Iversen, 2017; Prescott, 1996; Solheim, 2021). The FBC of Northern Germany and southern Scandinavia also developed early on into the first societies using and producing metalwork within this sphere (Gebauer et al., 2021).

The Middle Neolithic provides evidence for considerable micro-regional variation in animal husbandry. While sheep/goat, cattle, and pig become more visible during this time in some parts of Scandinavia, the transition from hunting to stock breeding is not established consistently until the turn to the LN in Norway and Eastern Middle Sweden (Solheim, 2021). This corresponds with a move to more permanent farmsteads with two-aisled longhouses around 2200 BCE in these areas, which evolves to the building tradition of tree-aisled longhouses during the Early NordicBA (c. 1600 BCE). Archaeobotanical data demonstrate that during these phases of the Neolithic, massive deforestation and the establishment of heathland along the coastal micro-regions of southern and middle Scandinavia took place. These major anthropogenic ecological changes shape these areas until today.

Two pivotal, large-scale events shaped the economic future of southern Scandinavia prior to the start of the Bronze Age. First was the introduction of a more pastoralist economy around 2800 BCE with the migration of groups with eastern step ancestry from which the local Corded Ware cultures emerged (Haak et al., 2015). Afterwards, the Atlantic Bell Beaker expansion introduced maritime and metal-based economies. This was perhaps linked to technological innovations such as advanced plank-built boats that could carry larger crews and more cargo (Ling, 2012; Melheim and Ling, 2017; Østmo, 2008). The Corded Ware and the Bell Beaker groups interacted with existing cultures, which eventually led to the local LN cultures fully adopting and integrating the innovations from 2100 BCE onwards (Artursson, 2009). It has been argued that the LN (2350–1700 BCE) marked the beginning of the Bronze Age before it completely manifested itself around 1800/1700 BCE (Apel, 2001; Artursson, 2015; Vandkilde, 1996).

Many factors contributed to the uniformity of the NordicBA, but a primary cause was the engagement of local communities with long-distance metal trade dependent on the new boat technology. This was driven by a social structure that favored peer-polity interaction and elite control (Earle et al., 2015; Kristiansen, 1987; Ling et al., 2018b). The relatively low-density population that upheld these systems is estimated to consist of c. 12–15 people per km^2 in the most densely populated micro-regions and four to six people in less dense areas. This equals a total population of c. 300,000–500,000 people in Scandinavia (see also Holst et al., 2013). Considering the topography and the geographic distribution of settlements, burials, hoards, and rock art, the presence of smaller polities, perhaps chiefdoms or similar formations expanding on average up to c. 400–800 km^2, can be postulated (Figure 2). Variations in size can be observed depending on whether they were coastal or inland. The emergence of more evident social hierarchies begins during the LN, which comes fully into its own during the Early Bronze Age (EBA), when all societies expressed social stratification in monumental burials, house sizes, metal wealth, and rock art. These hierarchies consisted of chieftains, warriors, and free farmers at the top followed by commoners and most likely slaves at the bottom. This system, recently named the maritime mode of production (Ling et al., 2018b), operated through a variety of strategies, including political control of agropastoral production, maritime trade, regional alliances, and violence.

The chronology of the NordicBA has been a focus of Scandinavian archaeology because of the early recovery and analysis of its dramatic bronze metalwork. Following Oscar Montelius' (1885) typology, the NordicBA was divided into an early and a late phase, with three periods each. Period I has been further subdivided (Figure 3). Since we also relate this book to northernmost Germany,

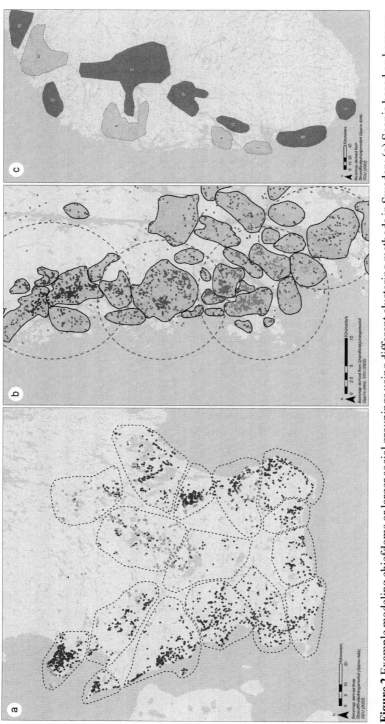

Figure 2 Example modeling chiefdoms or larger social groupings using different clustering methods in Sweden: (a) Scania based on barrows (dark) and cairns (yellow); (b) Bohuslän based on cairns and rock art (color represents different computed clusters); (c) Western Norway based on burials, settlement, daggers, simple shaft-hole axes, and sickles (yellow – clustered artifacts from Period III) (Produced by Ashely Green, data by the authors)

Dates	Scandinavia	Britain/ Ireland	Iberia	Central Europe	Italy	Greece
2400		Chalcolithic	Chalcolithic	Late Neolithic	Chalcolithic	
2300	LN I					
2200	Late Neolithic					
2100						Middle Bronze Age
2000	LN II		Early Bronze Age	Early Bronze Age	Early Bronze Age	
1900		Early Bronze Age				
1800						
1700	P Ia					
1600	P Ib					
1500	P II		Middle Bronze Age	Middle Bronze Age	Middle Bronze Age	
1400	Early Bronze Age	Middle Bronze Age				
1300	P III					Late Bronze Age
1200					Recent Bronze Age	
1100	P IV	Late Bronze Age	Late Bronze Age	Late Bronze Age		
1000					Final Bronze Age	
900	P V					
800	Late Bronze Age					Proto-Geometric
700	P VI		Iron Age			
600		Iron Age		Iron Age	Iron Age	
500	Iron Age					

Figure 3 Comparative chronology table

the beginning of the Bronze Age is set to 1800 BCE; in Scandinavia, this is usually dated to 1700 BCE (Vandkilde, 1996). The periodization of the NordicBA presupposes a typo-chronological uniformity across the entire region with only a few challenging this view (Müller, 1877). The division into six periods is nonetheless useful for arranging the NordicBA into more manageable culture-historical developments (Figure 3).

Period I (1800/1700–1500 BCE) represents the first import of copper and tin to cast objects locally. However, by 2000 BCE, some metals were imported from the Central European Únětice culture and the British Isles including some local recasting (Vandkilde, 1996; Wrobel Nørgaard et al., 2019). By 1600 BCE, we see the dominance of locally made bronze objects in the Nordic metalwork style. In Period II (1500–1300 BCE), the NordicBA comes into its own with unique types of swords, spiral ornamented metal objects (Horn, 2015), monumental earthen burial mounds and cairns, and large three-aisled longhouses (Artursson, 2009, 2015; Holst et al., 2013; Vandkilde, 2014). Swords, tutuli, and belt plates were among the distinctive metal objects that were widely distributed in Scandinavia often as burial goods in well-preserved oak log coffins (Holst et al., 2001). In Period III (1300–1100 BCE), which marks the end of the EBA, many elements first appearing during Period II continue, but now styles changed from spiral ornamentation to concentric circles on a variety of artifacts (Randsborg, 1969). In the archaeological record, Periods II and III stand out as the phases with the most metalwork finds. Therefore, they are considered important phases where communities engaged in extensive interregional contact networks including trade in metal, textiles, exotics, and slaves (Earle et al., 2015). This allowed individuals to expand their influence, and warriors became highly influential.

The transition to Period IV (1100–900 BCE) saw changes and turmoil, including the rise of a new burial custom, going from predominantly inhumation to cremation, which was influenced by the emerging Urnfield culture on the continent (Vandkilde, 2007). In the Mediterranean, the influential Mycenaean culture collapsed, sending shockwaves across Southern Europe and indirectly affecting trade networks to Northern Europe and Scandinavia. Resource-demanding building activities, like monumental burials and large longhouses, end, perhaps related to a resource crisis in grazing land and timber (Holst et al., 2013; Kristiansen, 2010). Yet, kinship ties, aggrandizement of local elites, historical relatedness, for example, in the many secondary cremation burials in EBA barrows, and elaborated warrior depictions in rock art, still play a part in the social structure. Metal was continuously supplied as compared to previous periods even more extravagant and bronze demanding artifacts were produced, like the helmets from Viksø (Figure 4) (Vandkilde et al., 2022).

During Period V (900–700 BCE), all features present continued in elaborated form, including increased ritual depositions in lakes and bogs (Myhre, 1998). In Period VI (700–500 BCE), the Hallstatt culture was well established on the continent, with imports reaching Scandinavia. By now, Central Europe had largely entered the Iron Age, and in Scandinavia, locally made iron objects emerged in the archaeological record. At the end of the Late Bronze Age (LBA), Scandinavia transitioned into the Pre-Roman Iron Age (500–0 BCE). Developing out of the Hallstatt culture, the La Tène culture with its intricate bronze and iron objects dominated Central and Western Europe. Conflict on the continent interrupted trade routes and forced Scandinavia to use its locally plentiful iron sources. Archaeologically less clear-cut hierarchical organization forms, that is, farmsteads, seem more independent of each other in some locations, but small villages developed elsewhere. With the "international" Bronze Age now gone, the emerging Scandinavian Iron Age was quite locally oriented, and it was not until the Viking Age (AD 790–1050) that the expansive chiefly maritime confederacies emerged to their full potential once more (Ling et al., 2018b).

Figure 4 Helmets from Viksø (photo by the National Museum of Denmark, CC BY-SA 3.0)

The NordicBA witnesses the development of a characteristic complexity that appears to have rested on a distinctive economy involving a specialization in seafaring within the maritime spheres of the Baltic Sea, the North Sea, Skagerrak, and Kattegat, but also along rivers, fjords, and across the large inland lakes (Ling et al., 2018b; Nimura et al., 2020). Cultivation of cereals, animal husbandry, and, to some degree, hunting, fishing, and gathering constituted a self-sustaining economic base and produced a surplus that could be used for investments in monuments, ships, and metal (Prescott, 2012). This allowed participation in local, regional, and interregional exchange networks, but also enabled central regions to control flows and distributions of goods for their own gain (Kristiansen, 2007).

The sociopolitical and cultural changes beginning around 1800/1700 BCE were profound, and they arguably represent one of the most pivotal phases in European prehistory (Kristiansen, 2000; Prescott, 1994). Not only do we see new formalized political systems but also technological innovations like the three-aisled longhouse and the sword that would last well into the medieval period (Eriksen and Austvoll, 2020; Kristiansen, 2007; Molloy and Horn, 2020). Such innovations led to an increase in surplus production which resulted in a more predictable, expanded, and stable economy (Iversen, 2017).

Throughout the NordicBA, domestic and political economies, regardless of their specific local setup, were strongly oriented toward seafaring operating within the MMP (Section 2). This led to processes of regional alignment, for example, the forming of alliances, and divergence, for example, competition. These were not static, but communities were probably always shifting alliances and creating new adversaries which would have changed the political landscape rapidly. While this may seem contradictory in the grand narrative of NordicBA uniformity, it is understandable when we consider that each community had self-sufficiency as self-interest informed by individual and communal decision-making which may or may not have been in line with the self-interest of polities near and far. Therefore, our text always centers on local societies to understand the bigger picture because it is the constant economic interaction of local communities, and thus contact, that caused the outward uniformity of the NordicBA.

2 Macroeconomic Perspectives

Our analysis is based on a distinctive set of economic conditions found in the NordicBA that includes farm- and boat-based primary economic units, local adaption to contrasting economies, and the formation of a macroeconomy that supported the emergence of a political economy that spread across the region and led to the development of observable emergent complexity. In this section, we highlight some of the theoretical models used to interpret Bronze Age societies and their economies followed by a discussion of our theoretical approach. Several approaches have been proposed to describe Scandinavia's role within the macroeconomic system of Bronze Age Europe in which it was often framed as a peripheral area. However, it can be shown that it was an embedded and active participant in the Bronze Age European world with a high demand for metal and other exotic goods.

The macroeconomic approach that we put forward for the NordicBA has a long history that is useful to briefly review. Since the late nineteenth century, cultural changes in Scandinavia have been understood as having diffused from the East, making typological comparison with far regions such as Egypt (Montelius, 1881, 1885; Müller, 1888, 1909). In the early to mid-twentieth centuries, macroeconomic views were used to synthesize the culture-historical development of European prehistory (Childe, 1925, 1931, 1951), which inspired Scandinavian scholars (Åberg, 1930–1935; Broholm, 1944; Kristiansen and Larsson, 2005). However, by the 1960s, in the early days of the New Archaeology, research became more concerned with internal develop-ments of groups, reacting to nationalistic archaeologies like Gustav Kossinna's

Siedlungsarchäologie (Trigger, 2006). A move away from macro-regional frameworks effectively ended migration and mobility as explanatory models. Instead, scholars emphasized internal system-oriented dynamics (Binford, 1962; Clarke, 1971). NordicBA research became more functionalistic as local and micro-regional developments were prioritized (Baudou, 1960; Bakka, 1963; Bakka and Kaland, 1971; Hagen, 1983; Marstrander, 1963; Møllerop, 1962; Randsborg, 1969). Evert Baudou's (1960) seminal work exemplifies an emphasis on regionality; although importing metal into Scandinavia was known to be a critical factor, only southern Scandinavia was thought affected, while more northern regions were seen as localized, peripheral hunter–fisher communities (Amundsen, 2017). The long-running dual-culture debate illustrates this for Norwegian Bronze Age research (Brøgger, 1925; Gjessing, 1945; Hagen, 1983), where a proper Bronze Age was seen as limited to a few areas in South Norway with few dissenting voices arguing that the Bronze Age was a shared cultural and socioeconomic perception stretching across Scandinavia (Shetelig, 1925).

During the 1970s and 1980s, Scandinavian scholars became more attuned to theoretical changes from the British Isles, and key concepts, like the peer-polity interaction model (Renfrew, 1974, 1986) and center-periphery perspectives (Wallerstein, 1974), were discussed by Michael Rowlands et al. (1987). These ideas became central for NordicBA research (Kristiansen, 1987; Larsson, 1989; Mandt, 1991; Prescott, 1991b). These macro-theories conceptualized social transformation as driven by external communication and interaction, and less as endogenous processes (Champion, 1989; Sherratt, 1993). Furthermore, concepts such as alliances and networks were seen as important to understand variations in socioeconomic development (Brumfiel, 1987; Brumfiel and Earle, 1987; D'Altroy and Earle, 1985; Earle, 1978; Feinman and Neitzel, 1984; Gilman, 1981). Importantly, for the Scandinavian Peninsula, the amount of metal became less important; rather, interaction between societies of unequal scale and status became a prime mover for understanding the sociopolitical development of the NordicBA. Specifically, several different political economy approaches investigated the relationship between power, economy, and social spheres through the Marxian principal that various social segments in society have individual goals and wishes that oppose each other, which can be maneuvered and exploited strategically by the upper social strata for their own economic gain (Earle, 2019).

With the introduction of the ethnohistorical concepts of chiefdoms, researchers began to outline more dynamic understandings of the NordicBA. Scholars such as Kristian Kristiansen, Henrik Thrane, Helle Vandkilde, Christopher Prescott, and Thomas Larsson addressed aspects of the NordicBA beyond limited regional studies or specific source categories (Kristiansen, 1989; Larsson, 1986; Prescott, 1995; Thrane, 1998; Vandkilde, 1996). Kristiansen (1987) aimed to readdress the relationship between South Scandinavian centrality and the peripheral northern regions through a multicontextual top-down analysis. He argued against a major dichotomy between Scandinavian microregions in terms of subsistence economy and social organization; rather, he considered it to be a question of degree (compare Shetelig, 1925). This approach defined interdependent networks of alliances and trade as crucial for understanding the NordicBA.

The post-processual critique of the sometimes overly functionalistic views of processualism during the 1990s and early 2000s also affected NordicBA research. Added focus on cosmology and religion, theoretical cues from the social sciences and a return to more locally oriented research dominated this new paradigm (Goldhahn, 1999; Larsen, 1997; Myhre, 2004; Skoglund, 2009). Important points from post-processualism were the emphasis on historical situatedness and its critique of society as a self-regulatory system found in early processualism. More recently, we are moving into what Kristiansen (2014) has termed the third-science revolution, reflected by the recent surge in scientific papers that implement aDNA, isotopes, and computing of big data. This has reignited older theories by Gordon Childe and Marija Gimbutas on migration and mobility in the Neolithic and Bronze Ages (Allentoft et al., 2015; Frei et al., 2017; Haak et al., 2015). From this emerged new theoretical strands that harken back to parts of processual archaeology and its emphasis on social organization (Earle et al., 2015; Kristiansen, 2016b; Ling et al., 2018b). Collective action theory is one of the emerging post-Marxist frameworks that have gotten traction in recent research (Austvoll, 2021; Lund et al., 2022). It "posits rational social actors who regularly assess the actions of others to inform their own decisions to cooperate" (DeMarrais and Earle, 2017). Others, like Vandkilde (2016), have drawn on World System Theory by Wallerstein (2011), for example, introducing the term "bronzization" when discussing early globalization during the Bronze Age. This is used to describe the global impact bronze as a resource had on societies in many parts of the Afro-Eurasian landmass, including a strong connectivity between disparate regions.

With this intellectual history in mind, we lay out our economic approach to understand two linked processes: (1) farm self-sufficiency with local adjustments to specific environmental conditions and (2) the convergence of networks of micro-regional systems with an emerging world economy involving metal trading and raiding. To understand the subsistence base of the NordicBA economy, we start with the concept of self-sufficiency that can be considered cross-culturally at three scales of integration – the household, the community, and the micro-regional polity. Local NordicBA economies comprised decentralized farms with local and regional investments in maritime technologies involving long-distance trade of metals. The key question is the degree to which groups at each level were economically independent, meaning that they produced what they needed. From an elemental level, we know that some interdependency existed in all societies, which is expressed by the nature and number of consumables in food, technology, and wealth objects coming from outside each unit. For example, for an individual community that we consider, we could say that a household produced 90 percent of its food and 60 percent of its basic technology like ceramics and flint tools but almost none of its prestige goods (Section 6). A similar analysis could be applied to both the local community and the micro-regional polity. The differences that we observe cross-culturally probably represent significant contrasts in political economies and strategies.

Focus on self-sufficiency of the farm unit relates to Karl Polanyi's concept of the householding unit (ranging from the peasant farm to the rural feudal estate) as both a producer and a consumer. Householding meant self-sufficiency, and he identified it as the basic "principles of behavior" anchoring economy in social organization, alongside reciprocity and redistribution, prior to the advent of commercial exchange (Polanyi, 2001). Marshall Sahlins (1972) developed these issues further coining notions about the domestic mode of production. Three primary aspects may be used to summarize this concept: family labor force divided by gender and age, basic technology, and limited production targets based on maintenance of the household. A related but less specific model is Marx and Engel's Germanic mode of production (GMP) (Engels, 1942; Marx, 1953), in which the political economy was agrarian-based and highly decentralized. The GMP consisted of autonomous households that formed independent production units (Gilman, 1995; Marx, 1953), coalitions of households were further organized in tribal assemblies, and hereditary leadership was based on military and judicial activities. This is a model that is well represented by the NordicBA and its longhouse tradition (Artursson, 2009, 2015; Earle et al., 2022).

Building on the concept of independent farms, our model of NordicBA considers how networks of complementarity within and between different regional economies created the MMP (Ling et al., 2018b). This model helps to understand a path to institutional formation in decentralized chiefdoms with low population densities, mobile warriors, and long-distance trading/raiding for valuables, weapons, and slaves.

It is important to distinguish between the political economy and the domestic economy before we define the MMP further and connect it to concepts of

self-sufficiency and comparative advantage. Political and domestic economies are strongly interdependent (Figure 5), but they represent different
strategies and objectives (Earle, 2002). The domestic economy encompasses
a variety of productive activities carried out by domestic units, that is,
households and communities to provide resources for biological and cultural
reproduction. The NordicBA political economy, on the other hand, was
predicated on elites extracting surpluses to support their agendas and institutions, for example, to fund various expeditions, monumental construction,
finance attached specialists, build public works, and so on. In this view, the
political economy was built on productive surpluses that extend beyond what
the domestic unit needed for biological or cultural reproduction (Earle, 2002).

The primary question at hand is how the domestic and political economies
can be connected to self-sufficiency in terms of the household, the community,
and the micro-regional polity. The reason to maintain self-sufficiency was the
ability to fulfill one's own objectives without reliance on others, whom one
cannot fully control. In contrast, the most obvious reasons to engage with
outside actors involved comparative economic advantages (Ling et al., 2018b;
Ricardo, 2004) between households, communities, and micro-regions based on
their differing access to resources, knowledge, and technology. Key factors
determining comparative advantages among economic units included environmental advantages, the freedom of movement, ownership of resources, and
technologies of transport. Each can be seen as a transaction expenditure making
economic dependency more costly.

The reliance on distant movements of goods offered opportunities for control
of bottlenecks in economic flows such as the ownership of boats (Ling et al.,
2018b). Maritime raiding and trading in the NordicBA were conducted by low-
density agrarian societies, in which farmstead self-sufficiency was a rule.
Chiefly farmsteads, however, were able to control larger areas and intensify
production with additional labor to generate surpluses that chieftains used to
control a political economy based on wealth-finance derived from distant
maritime expeditions, raids, and the accumulation of metal wealth.
Scandinavian societies were the great raider-traders of the North Atlantic during
this time, with their economy resting upon the MMP as summarized in the
following:

- Exchange of wealth interconnecting low-density populations
- Warriors that raid, trade, protect, and intimidate
- Farming of productive lands by autonomous households owned by free
  farmers and chieftains
- Slave labor to expand surplus production and as an exchange commodity

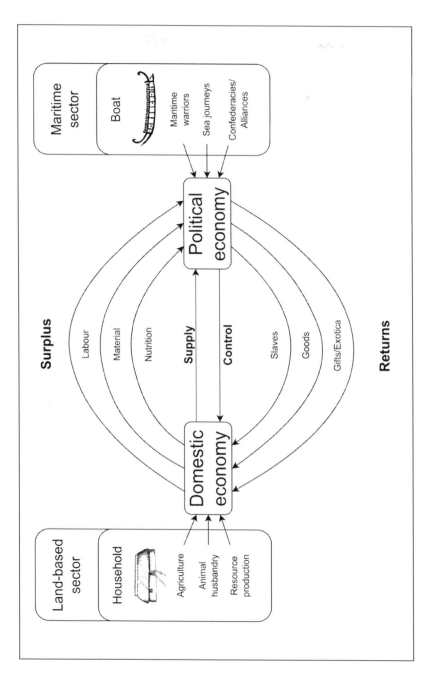

Figure 5 Integration of domestic and political economies in the maritime mode of production (created by Christian Horn)

- Maritime sector with specialized knowledge of boatbuilding and navigation
- Chiefly ownership of boats by funding their construction
- Raiding for slaves and other valuables along voyaging routes
- Chiefly control over returns such as metal or slaves through ownership of boats and supporting expeditions
- Redistribution, for example, gift exchanges established chiefly networks of power and alliances

Characteristics of the MMP that were particularly relevant to Scandinavia were the specific interaction between the domestic and political economies (Figure 5). This is exemplified by the presence of two key sectors, that is, the land-based agropastoral sector connected to individual farmsteads and the sea-based maritime sector connected to the boat unit. To participate in trade networks and warfare, Scandinavian groups depended on both sectors, but, because of social and environmental differences, some regions specialized more in one or the other.

The result was a division of labor and comparative advantages between regions with varied forms of environments and social settings that ranged from coercive to cooperative social organization (Austvoll, 2021; Feinman, 2017). Coercive groups used the wealth generated by their large-scale agropastoral activities to invest in long-distance exchange (Austvoll, 2020). Cooperative communities often located more inland and in mountainous regions, but also occasionally in coastal areas, were forced to resort to a more diverse economy, which included agropastoralism along with hunting, fishing, and timber extraction. For this latter strategy to succeed, increased cooperation would have facilitated trade which was essential for survival (Austvoll, 2021). For example, the more cooperative social settings in coastal western Sweden and Norway had ample access to fish and timber, whereas timber was already scarce in some of the most densely populated agropastoral micro-regions of Denmark (Ling et al., 2018b). The latter had more coercive social settings and clear comparative advantages in terms of agropastoral production, which in turn led to an accumulation of wealth and power reflected in metal consumption (Kristiansen, 2000). It created opportunities for elites to create confederacies of exchange and control over prestige goods which transformed these societies into expansive political machines (Earle et al., 2015).

Archaeological data point to high sufficiency for farms, communities, and micro-regional polities with both coercive and cooperative social relations. Due to the relatively limited evidence of hamlets and villages, the NordicBA exhibits a high degree of farm independence, as well as local and micro-regional investments in nautical technology, including long-distance metal trade.

However, the variation in settlement organization and density was great (Artursson, 2009, 2015). To concretize and illustrate variations in how the MMP was locally formulated, we consider archaeological evidence of interaction that linked these rather remote areas (Section 4), the different modes of such interaction (Section 5), and four contrasting cases from Denmark, Sweden, and Norway (Section 6).

3 The Domestic Economy

Resources for biological and cultural reproduction are produced in the domestic economy, a complex integrated system that provides nutrition, clothing, and materials for crafts through the exploitation of animals, plants, and other natural resources. Furthermore, the building tradition and the organization of farmsteads and settlements inform us about the social organization and capacity of production. This helps us to investigate landscape organization and relationships between farmsteads. Here, we discuss domestic economies of the NordicBA to understand significant investments that were made into buildings, settlements, and agriculture because they formed the agropastoral basis of local self-sufficiency and surplus production for the political economy (Figure 5).

3.1 Farmsteads and Settlement Organization

The organization of settlements provides strong and direct evidence of human relationships to landscapes. Excavations of individual farmsteads and their wider settled landscapes have contributed much to our understanding of how the domestic economy was structured and organized. However, for a long time, Scandinavian settlement archaeology was dominated by the paradigm that the common settlement pattern consisted of standardized, single farmsteads dominated by multifunctional longhouses inhabited by an extended family, in some cases supplemented by smaller economic buildings for storage and craftsmanship. The occasional existence of hamlet-like agglomerations of two or three such farmsteads was recognized, but underappreciated. Farmsteads were assumed to spread out relatively evenly throughout the landscape. Therefore, the general level of communication and cooperation between the individual farmsteads was assumed to be low (Artursson, 2009; Brink, 2013), continuing the LN settlement organization (Thrane, 2013). According to this paradigm, villages only occurred at the very end of the Bronze Age or in the Early Iron Age. Research on house building and settlement patterns has corrected this view by emphasizing greater local and micro-regional diversity in settlement structures including larger agglomerations of farmsteads in hamlets and small villages (Artursson, 2009, 2015).

Large-scale contract excavations have documented contemporary farmsteads in southern Sweden with good radiocarbon chronologies, for example, in Hyllie, outside of the modern city of Malmö. The excavated settlement area had a long period of stability from the Middle Neolithic B to Period III of the NordicBA. Within this settlement area, the locality Almhov stands out from the transition between LN I-II to the BA-IA transition, 2000–1600 BCE. Five to six contemporary farms clustered closely together forming a large hamlet. The farmsteads at Almhov, which can reach considerable sizes, were organized like other farmsteads in the micro-region with one main building and one or several smaller houses. Rebuilding histories of house upon house shows that families owned farmsteads across several generations (Brink, 2013, 2015).

The famous settlement Apalle in Uppland c. 50 km northwest of Stockholm demonstrated that Almhov was not an isolated case and that larger building agglomerations were not restricted to the south. Apalle was also settled for a long time from the Neolithic to the Iron Age. Settlement activity was concentrated in the Bronze Age with five main phases from 1300 to 500 BCE (Periods III–VI). The later phases had ten to twelve contemporary longhouses together with several smaller buildings. Evidence here suggests that Apalle was a center for production and distribution of metals and other high-status objects (Artursson, 2009; Ullén, 2003).

As a southern Danish example, the settlement in Højgård in Jutland had thirty-three buildings mainly dating to the EBA Periods I–III (Ethelberg, 2000). Five farmsteads have been identified, of which four appear contemporaneously (1600–1100 BCE) (Artursson, 2009). More sites on the Danish Isles qualify as hamlets or small villages such as the well-known settlement at Kirkebjerget, Fyn (Berglund, 1982). At Tietgen Byen on northern Fyn, twenty-nine buildings accumulated in an area of 12.35 ha (OBM8436) dating to the end of the LN and beginning Bronze Age (2000–1500 BCE) which increased to sixty-seven buildings during the LBA. Some farmsteads had adjacent smaller buildings (Runge, 2012).

The southwestern coast of Norway was often regarded as a periphery, but here too indications of occasional settlement agglomerations exist. In Tjora, Rogaland, five out of seven unearthed longhouses dating between 2000 and 1500 BCE may have been contemporaneous. Between 1500 and 1100 BCE, settlement activity in the area seems to decline (Fyllingen, 2012). Other important micro-regions like Bohuslän, western Sweden, with its many rock art sites, have not yet produced similar settlement agglomerations.

In most cases, farmsteads in hamlets were located about 50–100 m apart. Living so close together must have required cooperation, for example, in agriculture. House proximity and building over generations necessitated social cohesion, for example, in agreeing on land ownership of the different houses. Since it was often not possible to have agricultural land in the limited spaces between the farmsteads, parceling out of fields and pastures must have been planned, discussed, and protected by verbal contracts. This also implies that issues were resolved by commonly accepted rules and regulations which were probably based upon local customs and traditions. Almhov, Tietgen Byen, Apalle, Bjerre, and perhaps Tjora showed that this model successfully dominated their immediate surroundings for extended time periods, and sometimes centuries (Artursson et al., 2017; Brink, 2013, 2015).

3.2 Hierarchies of Farmsteads

Individual farms were the building blocks of the NordicBA economy that engaged in production of livestock and cereal crops. In archaeological research, buildings were typically classed by their interior space as large buildings with over 200 m^2, medium buildings with 85–130 m^2, and small buildings with 50–70 m^2. Generally, their internal space ranged from 50 to 500 m^2 with lengths of 10–50 m. From the LN throughout the EBA, house sizes were increasing (Figure 6). With the full breakthrough of the NordicBA

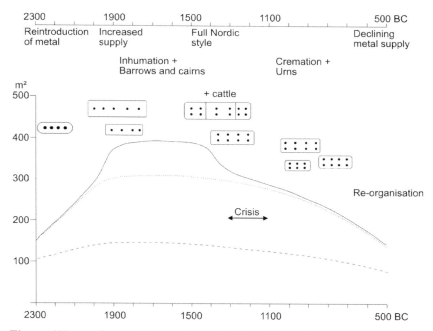

Figure 6 House sizes and layout during the NordicBA with major contemporary events indicated (after Magnusson 2009, adapted by Christian Horn)

around 1600 BCE, the large longhouses became very big, increasing overall differences in house sizes. Also, during this time, the roof-bearing construction of longhouses changed from two aisles (one row of central supporting roof posts) to three (two rows), which afterwards remained the prevalent construction form. At the end of the EBA, longhouse sizes began to decrease again, and the tradition of the extraordinarily large buildings disappeared (Artursson, 2009; Kristiansen, 2006). The largest longhouses at each site probably served as living quarters for local leaders. Apart from differences in economic and social power, the different sizes of longhouses were also indicative of environmental restraints like resource availability, the workforce that could be organized, building traditions, and so on. Additional buildings were perhaps constructed depending on these families' needs and opportunities.

The early increase in house sizes has been interpreted as an increase in social stratification. Ethnographically, large houses in stratified societies were a way for high-status families to demonstrate their economic power to gain even more influence. Prentiss et al. (2008) observed that members of impoverished families in British Columbia were incorporated into richer households as subservient labor which enabled these high-status families to invest in increasingly larger houses. The presence of specialized weapons, rich metalwork, and ritual depositions indicates that the LN in Scandinavia was already stratified (Horn, 2014; Vandkilde, 1996) and the same applies to the LBA (Kristiansen and Larsson, 2005) despite house sizes being more equal and, on average, smaller than during the EBA. Therefore, what we see during the EBA is most likely a shift in the customs to express power (Figure 6). A similar pattern has been observed for associated barrows that reinforced likely patterns of inheritance of status and land (Ling et al., 2018b).

Considerable variation existed in longhouse sizes throughout the Nordic sphere. A study of longhouses in Bohuslän dating to 1400–500 BCE found that sizes vary between 39 and 168 m^2 (Streiffert, 2004), which means those longhouses did not reach the sizes of longhouses on Jutland, the Danish Isles, or southwest Sweden. In addition, the settlements in Bohuslän clustered closely to the coast, whereas in Denmark, they spread far inland. In Western Norway, houses were smaller than in Denmark but larger than in Bohuslän, and with a similar coastal spread. The largest longhouse in northwest Scandinavia was discovered at Kleppe, Rogaland, with up to 225 m^2 dating to 1700–1500 BCE (Austvoll, 2021: 55). Along the western Norwegian coast, the peak in house size difference was reached between 1300 and 1100 BCE and was most pronounced in Rogaland, whereas in Denmark and southern Sweden the same happened earlier, between 1500 and 1300 BCE.

Researchers have recognized subdivisions inside longhouses, mostly within the living area in the western part of the structures. The best observed cases are longhouses from Legaard (Denmark) with plank walls dating between c. 1400 and 1250 BCE. They had two living quarters each, one in the west and one in the east. There is an ongoing debate about who inhabited these compartments, but it is agreed that each building housed a high-status family (Mikkelsen and Kristiansen, 2018). Despite the proximity of these longhouses to each other, the families seemingly did not feel the need to compete and outdo each other with the size of their homes. These longhouses were built shortly before house size declined (Artursson, 2009). Beginning in Period II in Denmark, a shortage of timber probably contributed directly to declining house sizes (Mikkelsen and Kristiansen, 2018; Olsen and Earle, 2018). This is supported by the observation that peat not wood was used as fuel, and inferior construction wood was used for repairs and house extensions like at Legaard or Bjerre. The crisis made timber too costly to construct ever-larger buildings. The use of rare timber would probably have been ideal to indicate power and prestige. Thus, while the declining house size differences may indicate declining social stratification, it is more likely-based on other evidence like rock art-that the customs to express power differences shifted during the LBA.

In summary, house construction in the Nordic sphere depended on local resource availability, population density, local competition, and customs. For example, Western Norway probably never suffered the same shortage of timber that befell Jutland, allowing house sizes to increase until the end of the EBA. It means that while general trends applied transregionally, lower population density areas had, on average, smaller longhouses which, in turn, could indicate a self-propelling process in micro-regions with larger populations, which led to more competitors requiring larger houses to assert dominance. This, in turn, required more surplus production leading to increasingly large populations, eventually propelling the crisis at the end of the EBA.

3.3 Animal Husbandry, Fishing, and Hunting

Domesticated animals and wild resources provided an essential, although variable, component of household economies during the NordicBA. Wild game and fish were not generally important, although notable exceptions existed. Faunal remains from the EBA are relatively scant, which may have to do with the Scandinavian acidic soil conditions, depositional practices, or taphonomy. However, recently, the available archaeozoological data has grown, especially from the LBA. During the EBA, the domestic economy was mostly based on cattle, for example, at Almhov

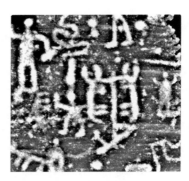

Figure 7 Rock art plowing scene in Finntorp (Tanum 90:1), Bohuslän, Sweden (laser scan by Henrik Zedig, visualization https://tvt.dh.gu.se/)

(Brink, 2015). The settlements in Bjerre represent some of the largest samples of bones of domesticated species in the entire Nordic zone and it shows a particularly strong reliance on cattle (Nyegaard, 2018). Skeletal changes indicate not just meat production but also a use as traction animals for plows or carts, as can be seen in the rock art of Sweden and Norway (Figure 7). The slaughtering of calves shortly after their birth indicates specialized strategies to increase milk production. Both strategies represented substantial economic investments but also risks, as any of the animals could have died before their prime, that is, the oxen before they could be used for traction, the dairy cattle before they could produce milk, or breeding animals before they reproduced.

By 1500 BCE, when three-aisled longhouses were regularly built, a new, more labor-intensive farming economy with better controlled land management based on animal wealth had been fully established in southern Scandinavia (Kristiansen, 2006), and human–animal relationships had perhaps changed significantly (Rasmussen, 1999). The internal structure of three-aisled longhouses may have formed byres for livestock, probably mainly cattle. Clear traces of such constructions were quite common in Thy and southern Jutland (Bech et al., 2018), for example, in Bjerre Enge and Legaard (Mikkelsen and Kristiansen, 2018; Nyegaard, 2018); however, they were missing in Sweden and Norway perhaps because of different animal husbandry strategies (e.g., Oma, 2018).

Dung from stalled cattle may have been used to manure fields. Phosphate analyses conducted in two houses in Legaard suggested that byres were cleaned, and dung distributed outside one of the entrances (Mikkelsen and Kristiansen, 2018). However, at Bjerre 4 little if any manuring was practiced (Dalsgaard and Nielsen, 2018). Carbon and nitrogen isotopic analysis has been used to estimate soil health and has indicated that some manuring was practiced during the

Neolithic and became more prevalent during the LBA but was insufficient to maintain soil fertility. Thus, its part to contribution agricultural output was negligible (Gron et al., 2021).

The need to protect livestock from raids could have been a contributing factor for stalling animals inside buildings (Section 5). It may also reflect gradual climatic cooling as more bodies would have helped to keep buildings warmer. During the LBA, the cattle dominated economy shifted toward a stronger presence of sheep/goat (Kristiansen, 2006), although herds were probably relatively small. Throughout the Bronze and Iron Ages, cattle herding appears to have been more concentrated at chiefly farms, likely rooted in the EBA development of cattle as a basis for wealth and status.

Throughout the NordicBA, variation in animal husbandry existed even within core zones perhaps to gain a comparative advantage to enable farmers to participate in exchange networks. The inhabitants of house 6 ("warrior house") in Bjerre relied to a degree on cattle and had, relatively speaking, fewer sheep/goats compared to the inhabitants of house 2 (see Earle et al., 1998). Some sites produced larger amounts of dog bones. However, dogs did not regularly provide sustenance but were mostly work and companion animals (Oma, 2018). Dog bones in houses were usually interpreted as ritual deposits, house offerings, to symbolically protect inhabitants.

Pigs played a minor role in the NordicBA subsistence economy but increased during the LBA. Cairn 10 in Nibble (Sweden) contained a surprisingly high amount of pig bone (Artursson et al., 2011). The monument was constructed by piling up fire-cracked stones covering an LBA burial. Pigs had likely greater relevance for the ritual economy rather than everyday nutrition. Perhaps pork was food reserved for higher classes in society or for special occasions. During Periods IV and V, the burials at Kumla (Uppsala, Sweden) near lake Hjälmared contained only sheep/goat bones, whereas the contemporary pit complex was dominated by bones of the common bream and other freshwater fish (Persson et al., 2002). This means fishing has contributed most to the subsistence at Kumla, and sheep/goat was perhaps preserved for feasts on special occasions.

Even more variation in animal use was observed in other micro-regions, such as coastal Hordaland in Western Norway. The Bronze Age occupation of the rock shelters at Ruskeneset, Rundøyno, and Skipshelleren show that domesticated animals, while being part of the local economy, only played a minor role (c. 16–38 percent) with a preference for sheep/goat rather than cattle. A substantial part of the local subsistence economy depended on hunting, mostly deer. The inhabitants of Ruskeneset also hunted seals and whales and relied on marine fish, mainly Atlantic cod and saithe, and, to a lesser extent, Atlantic pollock, ling, and mackerel. Skiphelleren was located further inland along the fjord, and faunal assemblages there contain much more saithe than cod which could also indicate that this rock shelter was used at different times of the year. There was apparently no exchange of foodstuffs such as fish judging by the exclusive exploitation of local resources, that is, marine species in Hordaland and exclusively freshwater species at the inland site of Kumla (Hufthammer, 2015). Osteological remains from Bohuslän indicate that fish were more abundant there than domestic animals (Ling, 2014). A cultural layer discovered on Orust included a bronze fishing hook and numerous fish bones from pollack cod, herring, and mackerel. That fishing also played some role in the local domestic economy further south is indicated by the presence of fishing hooks in burials. In addition, fish and fishing scenes occurred on metalwork and in rock art, for example, in Södra Ödsmål, Sweden, with two humans sitting in a boat operating three fishing lines.

3.4 Plant Agriculture

Our knowledge of plant use has increased significantly with flotation on modern excavations (Earle et al., 2022). The data indicate that agriculture produced a critical part of nutrition with surpluses supporting a wide range of activities. For example, farmhouses at Bjerre, which were preserved under drifting sands, sat among agricultural fields that appear to have been intensively farmed (Bech et al., 2018).

Barley (*Hordeum vulgare*) and emmer (*Triticum dicoccum*) remained stable crops throughout the entire region with some local variation (Effenberger, 2018). Whereas in Northern Germany, naked barley (*Hordeum nudum*) decreased in importance after the Neolithic, and it remains the most important cereal in Denmark, while hulled barley was less important. The southwestern micro-regions of Sweden and Norway do not match the cereal pattern of neighboring areas having a strong presence of hulled and naked barley, seemingly a mix between traditions in Schleswig-Holstein and Jutland (Effenberger, 2018; Prøsch-Danielsen and Soltvedt, 2011). In southwestern and southeastern Sweden, *Triticum aestivum* was relatively strong. With the beginning of the LBA, cereals became more varied, especially in southerly areas with the larger-scale use of broomcorn millet (*Panicum miliaceum*) (Effenberger, 2018; Stika and Heiss, 2013). Surprisingly, this was the case in southwestern Sweden rather than Jutland. Perhaps originally a weed, oat (*Avena* sp.) cultivation may also have begun during the LBA. Foxtail millet (*Setaria italica*) was probably not a cultivated crop but may have been traded.

Oily plants are more difficult to assess, but some trends have emerged. During the LBA, the oil plant spectrum may have widened with gold-of-pleasure

(*Camelina sativa*) and flax (*Linum usitatissimum*) being of equal importance (Henriksen et al., 2018). However, flax was perhaps used since the LN in Northern Germany (Effenberger, 2018). The earliest flax seed in Denmark was discovered in Bjerre Enge in house 3 dating to Periods II and III, but it was considered an intrusion that was brought here with other seeds.

Innovations in stable crop production were seemingly transmitted from south to north, although southwestern Sweden had perhaps direct contacts with southern micro-regions, as suggested by the presence of hulled barley and broomcorn millet. Sea travel could have facilitated such contact while avoiding intermediate areas. The widening and diversification of the stable crop production during the LBA was perhaps linked to depletion and health degeneration of the soil (Gron et al., 2021). Along with deforestation and overgrazing, decreasing soil fertility may have contributed to the crisis at the end of the EBA (Holst et al., 2013). The scale of this crisis and whether it was felt in areas like Bohuslän or Mälardalen is unclear. However, throughout the region, cultivars were diversified to maintain the domestic subsistence economy. Different ratios of crops indicated that at least on a regional scale, different strategies were employed (Regnell and Sjögren, 2006). Bronze Age communities down to individual farmsteads took care of their domestic economic needs by interacting and collaborating with neighbors as the settlement structure suggests.

3.5 Community Self-sufficiency for the Domestic Economy

Self-sufficiency (Section 2.2) was basic to the NordicBA domestic economy. It centered on productive activities carried out by an agricultural sector which provided resources for subsistence as indicated by the archaeozoological and archaeobotanical record from household excavations. This economy required investments in labor, seeds, fodder for animals, wood, and so on. However, in the low-population and premonetary systems that existed in the NordicBA, farms must also have relied on others to maintain subsistence production and handle risks that posed existential threats to the farmstead. Several interhousehold strategies to mitigate risk were practiced during the NordicBA, including networking through marriage, reciprocal exchanges, raiding, and other social ties (Sections 4–5).

Local communities employed different strategies to achieve self-sufficiency (Section 6) and micro-regions differed in some investments to maintain their domestic economies. While the construction of houses was important throughout the regions, marked differences existed in how boats served in domestic and political economies. Fishing was more essential in some regions, and boats were probably considerable investments for the domestic economy, for example, on

Orust, in Kumla (Sweden), or in Hordaland (Norway). Well-built and maintained boats increased the production for nutrition which also may have influenced the way boats were depicted in rock art.

3.6 Summary

The extended families that inhabited farmsteads followed an opportunistic strategy toward the self-sufficiency of the domestic economy. The major contributors were agriculture and herding. However, people in different microregions adapted to exploit local environments and the opportunities it provided. To secure a sufficient subsistence economy, several families may have banded together to pool their resources leading to temporal agglomerations of farmsteads. Occasionally, this may have led to more permanent hamlet- or villagelike structures sometimes persisting into the Iron Age. Apart from securing sociocultural reproduction and providing surplus for the political economy, the domestic economy also had an influence on beliefs, ideology, and cosmology as the different contexts of boat images indicated. All contributed to the richly varied domestic economies that can be observed in Scandinavia. The domestic economy described in this section was, of course, strongly interdependent with the political economy, but both involved different strategies and objectives (Earle, 2002). The political economy was predicated on the extraction of surplus in support of social institutions and the agendas of ruling entities, whether these were elites or forms of collective rulership (Section 6). This included but was not limited to funding monuments, acquiring exotic goods, financing attached specialists, building public works, and more.

4 Economic Interactions at Various Distances

Although farms were highly self-sufficient for subsistence, this was not true for many working tools, household utensils, and prestige items. It is, therefore, important to reflect on the resources needed by farms for production and personal display, and the distances that they were obtained at. Here we consider three spheres of exchange for goods and interaction: the micro-regions, the macro-regions, and long-distance contacts (Figure 8). Although these spheres were not distinctly drawn, the micro-region was perhaps within a day's journey by foot, horse, or boat. Most exchanges would be based on relationships of simple reciprocity between kin and neighbors, who knew each other intimately. Excavations at Bjerre suggest that such exchanges often involved higher quality flint tools, ceramics, some metals, and probably a range of archaeologically more elusive materials like leather, bone, and wood (Earle et al., 2022). Localized availability of better soils, higher quality of flints, suitable clays,

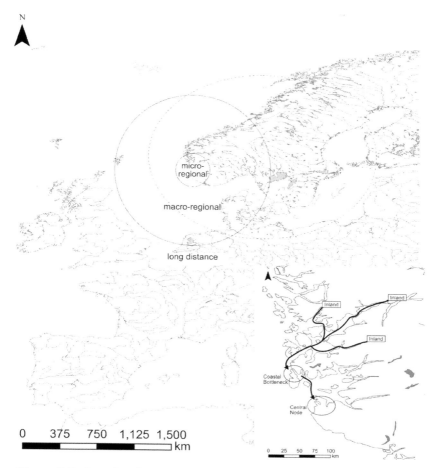

Figure 8 Scales of exchange represented by spheres of trade/interaction and distances including inland–coast relationships. The dotted circle indicates medium distances when considering cultural similarity, whereas the closed circle indicates absolute distances. The inset models local exchange on the example of Jæren (maps by Christian Horn and Knut Ivar Austvoll)

and the like may have contributed to part-time specializations of some farms. Their products, such as formal flint tools including daggers (LN), sickles, scrapers, strike-a-lights (EBA), knives (LBA), ceramics (LBA), metallurgy, and special wood working, could then have been exchanged primarily to neighboring farms, but also at longer distances. These economies were often structured through the local topography with farms being located along the coast or toward the hinterlands following rivers inland and in the north into the mountains. The coastal settlements of some micro-regions may have specialized in fishing and boatbuilding, while more inland farms concentrated on animal herding which required transhumance into the interior. Micro-regions in the NordicBA probably attempted to retained a high level of self-sufficiency among objects of everyday life and some for social distinction. We now consider more distant exchanges that involved resources and skills that were distinctive to micro-regions, and, thus, created systems of material flows with different social and political relationships.

4.1 Exchanges within the Cultural Region of Scandinavia

The wide expanse of the NordicBA required multiple days of travel, often by boat to traverse. The contacts among the travelers would have been somewhat less frequent and relationships less intimate than within micro-regions. Despite this, the cultural uniformity across the NordicBA suggests that networks of connections were well established, for example, for trade, marriage, and political alliances (Figure 8). Micro-regions within Scandinavia developed specialized production and exports using locally available materials, knowledge of their production, and skills in refining them. Materials traded across Scandinavia included specialty stones (flint, soapstone, slate, etc.), superior woods, resins and tar, metal, and probably many other materials that did not normally preserve or are under-researched. We can imagine that specialists in micro-regions with available special resources created interdependences based on trade that formed the networks of relationships, on which political coalitions were apparently formed.

Stones of high quality for special tools were not distributed evenly across Scandinavia. Specialization for extraction, manufacture, and trade is well documented (Varberg, 2005). Flint is the best known example which is restricted to southern Scandinavia (Jutland, Danish Islands, and Scania). In Denmark and southern Sweden, good evidence exists for the mining of high-quality flint for the specialized manufacture of formal tools, like daggers and sickles which were exported broadly (Apel, 2001). Such items were regularly discovered in the areas in Sweden and Norway where flint does not naturally occur.

Soapstone was also not uniformly distributed throughout Scandinavia. Similar to flint, soapstone sources varied in quality with some being usable for special purposes. For example, the production of good soapstone molds required quite specific qualities. Since sources for soapstone in Scandinavia did not coincide with locations at which soapstone molds have been discovered, regional trade can be inferred (Goldhahn and Østigård, 2007; Nilsson, 2011). Although it is currently not possible to pinpoint the location of sources for NordicBA soapstone finds, many of the high-quality sources were located relatively far north at some distance from the coast. Soapstone was, thus, a localized material, which northern and more inland communities could have produced for export. Trade likely involved coastal transport by boat, but, depending on source locations, transport could also have been carried along rivers, lakes, and fjords, which is indicated by finds between the lakes Vättern and Vänern in south-central Sweden.

The production of boats appears to have been localized in areas with lower-density populations than Jutland and access to suitable wood. As previously stated, during the EBA, much of the usable timber had been removed in the south to create fields and pastureland and perhaps for expanding use in pyro-technology. In coastal micro-regions like Bohuslän or southern Norway, a specialized maritime tradition is suggested by highly localized rock art hot-spots with over 20,000 boat images. The complexity of boat construction and the requirements for special materials must have made these locations nodes for economic exchange. Special materials included resin, tar, or pitch to tighten the vessels. Flax could also have been used to sew planks together. Additionally, boat construction required tools made from bronze, bone, antler, stone, and flint.

At least seventy tar, resin, or pitch loaves have been discovered in Scandinavia, of which many date to the Bronze Age (Bergström, 2004). Most have been found in Denmark and Sweden, but a few have also been discovered in Norway, for example, the two loaves from a bog in Ålberg, Nord-Trøndelag (Johansen, 1993). The NordicBA loaves were round with a small hole in the middle suggesting that multiple loaves were put on a rod or string together for transport (Figure 9). Their distribution was tightly linked to the coast, which suggests that they were transported by boat. Historical studies demonstrated that tar production required specialized knowledge from sourcing raw material to pyro-technology for the distillation of good quality material (Bergström, 2004). The analysis of residuals in ceramic vessels shows an increase in tar production during the NordicBA (Isaksson, 2009). The largest number of tarpots clustered in Mälardalen, Eastern Middle Sweden, but they are absent, for example, in Thy. However, evidence for tar use exists in the Danish burials (Figure 9).

Several Danish EBA burials in oak log coffins documented materials that rarely are preserved archaeologically but must have been traded regionally throughout Scandinavia (Figure 9). These oak coffins were produced from large trees that perhaps required to be traded from the north because they were not easily available in Denmark. The deceased had clothing made from linen and wool, both of special productions that suggest distribution over greater distances. Some coffins were wrapped with seaweed which required transport from the coast. The coffins and later LBA urns were sealed with resin or tar. The bodies themselves were wrapped in cattle hide. Specialization in the raising of

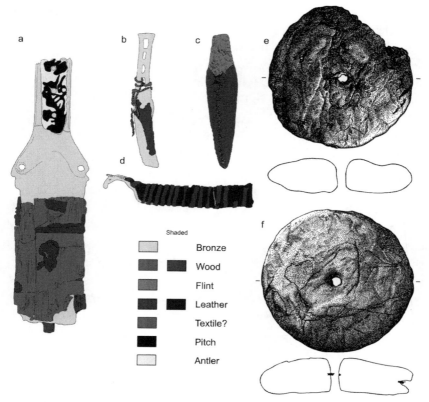

Figure 9 Multiresource objects: (a) sword from burial A in Bøvl, Sønder-Omme, Denmark (after Aner and Kersten 1990, No. 4457); (b)–(d) knife, flint dagger, and razor from a burial in barrow no. 17, Hvidegård, Lyngby-Tårbæk, Denmark (after Aner and Kersten 1973, No. 399); (e) and (f) two tar loaves potentially a hoard deposited in a bog or small lake in Ormslev, Denmark (after Aner and Kersten 2014, No. 6965; all redrawn by Christian Horn; no scale)

cattle and scraping of hides probably for trade was observed at Bjerre (house 6). Farms with available good pasturage might well have traded hides, for example, for tar, soapstone, or other high-quality products with the north, where conditions probably limited the number of cattle that could be raised.

Although much harder to document, salt has been one of the most traded commodities throughout world history. It serves many purposes, including daily intake to maintain health for humans and animals. It was used as preservative for foodstuffs due to its antimicrobial properties and, of course, as a seasoning to improve taste especially for special meals. Salt was produced by evaporation of salt water, burning of plants high in salt, and mining (Harding, 2017). In the

Bronze Age, notable discoveries include the salt mines in Hallstatt and elsewhere in the Austrian Alps. Technical ceramics called briquetage for salt evaporation have been found in Poland, Britain, France, the Iberian Peninsula, and in Germany as far north as Lüneburg. No evidence exists for salt production in the NordicBA proper, perhaps suggesting dispersed salt procurement from surrounding salt water and salt deposits at medium to long distances with Lüneburg being the closest known possibility which was culturally close to the NordicBA. The earliest evidence of salt production in Scandinavia dates to the Middle Ages (Harding, 2021).

4.2 Long-Distance Raiding, Trading, and Gift Exchanges

During the NordicBA, all copper and tin was imported into Scandinavia and evidently arrived first in locations that maintained access to water-based transport. Pyro-technic specialists then produced finished objects that were distributed throughout the region. The Bronze Age is often portrayed as a time of tightly guarded specialist metalworking and seafaring knowledge which was used to secure social status (Ling et al., 2018a). To understand the internal distribution of goods and the potential for inland communities to participate in economic interaction, other materials might be important including soapstone (Demange, 2012). Soapstone was used to carve molds for casting axes, swords, and other objects. Presumably, a greater number of molds would have been made from clay which could be sourced locally, although some pottery was also exchanged (Earle et al., 2022). The downside of clay molds is that they can only be used once because they have to be broken to retrieve the cast objects and they require a highly skilled worker for production. Soapstone molds, on the other hand, can be used up to fifty times (Nilsson, 2011). Two other advantages of soapstone in metal casting are that it can withstand temperatures of well over 1000 °C while only expanding minimally, which means it is heat shock resistant (Singer and Singer, 1963). In Thy, indications of small-scale LBA metalworking were found in household contexts associated with amber probably as an exchange item. During the EBA, evidence of metal production is more limited, suggesting production by specialists attached to and controlled by chiefly farms (Earle et al., 2022).

The focus of modern researchers has been on bronze in discussions of trading networks, but a diversity of other objects and materials was flowing through long-distance networks (Ling et al., 2018b). The log coffins with exceptional organic preservation portray a panoply of important materials (Holst and Rasmussen, 2013; Jensen, 2001) that most local communities would have depended on for a wide range of purposes (Hornstrup, 2017) including rituals, status expression, and daily production. With the short discussion in this section, we can begin to construct an ever more detailed interpretation of the complexity of economic interaction that NordicBA polities were involved in.

4.2.1 Copper and Tin for Bronze

Research on NordicBA economic interaction has been tightly linked to bronze, an alloy of copper and tin that was used to produce weapons and prestige goods. The long-distance procurement of these materials provided a key catalyst for the political economy forming hyper-regional connectivity that supported emergent complexity (Earle et al., 2015; Ling et al., 2017; Vandkilde, 2016). Its presence in burials and sacrificial depositions in addition to the near absence in settlements demonstrates its significance as a prestige and ritual material (Horn, 2018b). Bronze objects, especially weapons, were also overrepresented in Scandinavian rock art which further emphasizes the role of bronze in the NordicBA economy.

Micro-regions acquired copper and tin often from multiple sources. Lead isotope studies concentrating on NordicBA metalwork have demonstrated that several copper sources were accessed (Ling et al., 2014; Ling et al., 2019; Melheim et al., 2018; Nørgaard et al., 2019), and these sources changed through time and space. For example, swords from between 1600 and 1500 BCE found in Denmark often contain copper from the Great Orme mine in Wales, whereas no contemporary sword discovered in Sweden showed traces of this copper (Ling et al., 2019). During the earliest part of the NordicBA, fewer copper sources were used, like Wales, the Slovakian Ore Mountains, and Mitterberg in Austria. The range of sources gradually widened over time (Figure 1). Trade networks shifted to the south toward the Italian Alps around 1500 BCE and from 1300 BCE onward to the Iberian Peninsula and Sardinia (Ling et al., 2014, 2019; Melheim et al., 2018). Cornish tin was perhaps important throughout the entire Bronze Age but could have been supplemented from Iberian sources (O'Brien, 2015; Pernicka, 2010).

For 200 years, the Great Orme mine produced c. 4 tons of copper annually (Williams and Le Carlier de Veslud, 2019). Other mining sources, like the Mitterberg (Austria), have produced up to 20,000 tons in total or c. 66 tons per year (Pernicka et al., 2016). These estimates document that copper and tin were distributed as bulk goods in Europe. This was confirmed by the Uluburun ship, which sank c. 1300 BCE at the southern coast of Turkey. It carried oxhide and bun ingots totaling 10 tons of copper and 1 ton of tin (Pulak, 1998). Furthermore, the southern British Salcombe bay shipwreck produced 280 copper and 40 tin ingots. Complete ingots range between c. 300 and 1500 g with one tin ingot being an outlier with 9166 g (Wang et al., 2016; Wang et al., 2018). Finally, eighty additional finds of copper ingots have been made from several key maritime sites in England (Bradley, 2022; Cunliffe et al., 2019). This demonstrates that the British Channel was a trade nexus where European communities arrived by sea and exchanged copper and tin as well as other goods (Berger et al., 2022; Ling et al., 2014; Williams and Le Carlier de Veslud, 2019).

Estimates and numbers of ingots help to put the amount of copper in the NordicBA archaeological record into perspective. In the Nordic sphere, about 4000 swords, 1500 spearheads, 2000 daggers, and 4000 axes were produced mostly locally using bronze by highly skilled metallurgists. This represents 5500 specialized weapons and 6000 potential weapons, or a total of 11,500 implements with the potential to kill in close combat. This weaponry was frequently used in combat before it was deposited, suggesting that their direct link to actual warfare made them ideal ritual and status symbols, for example, as burial objects. Many weapons were sacrificed within a day's march to the coast and especially at important sea passages and transition zones indicating frequent, perhaps seasonal, raiding (Horn, 2016: section 5). Additionally, numerous pieces of jewelry and tools add to the consumption of copper and tin.

Published models estimated bronze availability to average c. 3 tons per year (Earle et al., 2015), which equals c. 100–150 g of bronze per year for a farmstead of ten to fifteen people (Rassmann, 2010). If 300,000–500,000 people divided between 50,000 farmsteads lived in Scandinavia between 1500 and 1400 BCE (Bunnefeld, 2018; Holst et al., 2013; Kristiansen, 2022), then these amounts of annually available metal is currently probably underestimated. For example, until the 1960s, only c. 20 spearheads of the type Torsted were known. The eponymous hoard in Torsted, after which the type was later named, alone contained forty of these spearheads packed tightly with seven flanged axes in a small stone cist (Figure 10) (Becker, 1964). Although the spears were not produced in the same mold, their similarity suggests that one workshop made them. That means a community close to Limfjord had the economic resources not only to produce forty-seven weapons in a short time but also to sacrifice and presumably replace them. This and similar finds suggest that many more weapons are missing in the archaeological record probably because they were never sacrificed (Horn, 2018a), which implies that NordicBA communities must have put a lot of effort into the exchange of copper and tin and that much more bronze was consumed than previously estimated.

4.2.2 Other Objects Moving at a Distance

Even though bronze was indubitably the most important material exchanged at a distance, other important resources can be documented. Exchanged as bulk

Figure 10 Torsted hoard: (a) Reconstruction drawing of the context (after Becker, 1964, by Rich Potter); (b) grinding striations underneath patina potentially related to repairs, magnification ×150; (c) blow mark on the midrib, magnification ×60; (d) weak indentation with slight replacement of material, magnification ×60 (photos by Christian Horn)

goods or as gifts, such things included locally, regionally, and distantly procured objects. Such exchange can either be reciprocal, that is, mutual giving and taking or negative reciprocal, that is, taking but not giving (Chernela, 2008; Sahlins, 1972: section 5). Most resources for technology, weapons, and personal display objects were unequally distributed, which means they needed to be sourced from a variety of regions across different physical distances and cultural settings. Different regions employed this unequal distribution to create comparative advantages of one region over another (Earle et al., 2015; Ling and Rowlands, 2013; Ricardo, 2004). To illustrate the diversity of exchanged materials, we consider amber and glass which are the best documented because of their survival in the archaeological record.

Amber is available locally across several regions in southern Scandinavia. It is a fossilized resin that washes out of the seabed especially after storms. The main source areas are the North Sea shore of Jutland into the estuary of the Elbe, southern Scania, and the southern Baltic Sea shore east of Lübeck to Finland (Dahlström and Brost, 1996). Amber was collected during the NordicBA, but it was only rarely crafted into beads for local use. It was rather a primary export to meet international demand from people to the south. Baltic amber has been found throughout Europe, for example, on the British Isles including the Wessex culture, and it was also present on Sark where copper ingots were deposited (Cunliffe et al., 2019). Amber was used by Central European cultures from the Únětice culture to the Urnfield culture. It was transported to the Iberian Peninsula in the west and to the Eastern Mediterranean Bronze Age cultures. Even in Syria and Egypt, where glass was produced, Baltic amber was present. Thus, we can assume that amber was an important raw material that some NordicBA communities collected for long-distance exchange (Harding et al., 1974; Mukherjee et al., 2008; Murillo-Barroso and Martinón-Torres, 2012; Odriozola et al., 2019; Woltermann, 2016).

Modern excavations of EBA house 6 and LBA house 7 in Bjerre have shed new light on the production and economic role of amber during the Bronze Age (Earle et al., 2022). In the "warrior house" 6, amber was collected perhaps to gain access to metal as found in household deposits. In commoner house 7, about 1800 pieces of amber were discovered, in some cases deposited in ceramic vessels dug into the floor, which had their openings easily accessible. This and other sites in Bjerre for sorting amber demonstrated that for the people living here, amber production was an everyday activity. Amber was not used for crafting locally in Bjerre and was likely treated as a raw material to engage in trade networks (Earle et al., 2022). Here we may be able to observe how a material transformed from being collected and perhaps exchanged in bulk into a gift at a distance. At its destination, it was rare and treated as a highly precious status symbol.

Glass production was not found in Scandinavia at this time. Glass beads were probably the most far-reaching import during the NordicBA. So far, only a limited number of ring-shaped glass beads (290) have been discovered dating to EBA (1400–1100 BCE). Color ranges from dark-blue and green to yellow and white. Most glass beads are monochromatic, that is, they have just a single color. Chemical analyses show that they were produced in Mesopotamia with two exceptions that were made in Egypt (Varberg et al., 2015, 2016). The shipwreck from Uluburun carried c. 200 glass ingots weighing c. 460 kg, which were likely produced in Egypt (Lankton et al., 2022). While this was not as heavy as the copper and tin freight, it indicates bulk exchange. This shipwreck represents only one cargo from one specific point in time during an era that spanned centuries. Most likely, many more similar cargoes were transported around the eastern Mediterranean Sea throughout the Bronze Age. Although it was contemporary to the NordicBA, most Scandinavian glass beads were not produced from glass like that carried by the Uluburun ship. However, similar sized cargoes of Mesopotamian glass may have existed. The beads deposited over c. 300 years of the NordicBA only weigh a few grams, which was a fraction of a single cargo. Thus, glass did not reach Scandinavia in bulk. Instead, the beads may have been an import of incredible luxury and/or the result of gift exchange. The importation of glass beads is fascinating because it occurs at a time when the locally available amber largely ceased to be used for beads. Thus, we may see a similar transformation from a bulk good into a gift, although with geographically speaking inverse directionality.

4.2.3 What Does Long-Distance Economic Interaction Mean in the Nordic Bronze Age?

The distance across which these foreign things moved required significant investments and offered opportunities for elite control. For longer journeys, more planning, proviant, and drinking water were required, gifts were needed to forge alliances, more repair materials needed to be carried, and more experienced sailors were required. Distance is directly linked to time and a significant labor force was missing for communities to work at farmsteads for a time that increased with the distance traveled (Ling et al., 2022). Copper, tin, gold, and glass come from outside the Nordic cultural sphere and were the subject of long-distance trade (Earle, 2002; Earle, 2010; Earle et al., 2015; Kristiansen and Larsson, 2005).

Despite the local availability of, for example, copper, flint, and clay, more distant sources were exploited perhaps because of lacking technological skills, relative quality of material, or shortages of labor needed to procure these resources locally. For some resources, we know the distances involved in their acquisition, even though knowledge is incomplete and imprecise (Ling et al., 2014; Melheim et al., 2018; Nørgaard et al., 2019). This is even more problematic for other resources. Most discussed possibilities become even more tenuous because communities may not have used the closest sources. With the discussion of bronze, an emphasis has been placed on political institutions and the political economy for the organization of journeys and actual travel in the service of long-distance trade, including the British Isles, the Alps, the Carpathian Basin, Iberia, and so on (Earle et al., 2015; Kristiansen and Larsson, 2005; Ling et al., 2018a; Vandkilde, 2016). However, it should be recognized that this is only half the story.

At the regional level of the NordicBA, the distances involved between micro-regions could be huge (Figures 1 and 8), that is, from Stjørdal in the north to lower Saxony in the south, it is roughly 1300 km as the crow flies. In such a large region, a boat journey from the settlement in Tietgen Byen on Fyn to the contemporary farmstead in Husby in Stjørdal (Norway) would have involved about 1600 km along the coast. Assuming speeds reached with a replica of the Early Iron Age boat from Hjortspring, the journey would have lasted c. 16–19 days. Travel times may have become considerably longer if the destination was further inland. A boat could be carried over some portages to reach the next navigable water body as it is sometimes depicted allegorically in rock art. However, some destinations may have been impossible to reach by boat, increasing transport costs significantly.

Distance and time for such journeys can be put in perspective by considering the English Channel which was called a nexus in the metal trade of Bronze Age Europe (Needham, 2009). On the former island of Thanet on Cliffs End (Kent, UK) isotopic evidence demonstrated that Iberian, British, and Scandinavian individuals came together during the LBA, perhaps to exchange raw metals and other resources (McKinley et al., 2014). Of course, we do not know precisely where these individuals lived, but we do know that they did cross the distance to Thanet. We could, for example, posit that some visitors came from the settlement at Tietgen Byen. The journey was about 1300 km or thirteen to fifteen days along the coastline. This means that this long-distance journey would actually be shorter than traveling from Husby to Tietgen Byen (Figure 1). Theoretically, soapstone or slate could have been acquired in Stjørdal. Even though it may be considered a culturally similar realm and no obvious high prestige goods like bronze were acquired, people still invested in such journeys because they also required other resources.

As discussed before, long journeys have a considerable cost, and for this reason, it seems unlikely that a single community could organize all journeys needed to acquire all required resources. Communities probably organized only a limited number of journeys to acquire enough goods to engage in micro-regional exchange. Under special circumstances, some may have acted as specialized traders. In the example discussed in this section, this may mean that individuals from Tietgen Byen may have traveled to Land's Cliffs End to acquire copper and tin from Iberia and Britain. They may have purposefully acquired more than they would have needed because they knew about people from Stjørdal, who would come with soapstone, slate, furs, or timber in exchange for metals. Of course, the directionality of such trade networks is inherently problematic to ascertain. However, the discussed principles may have applied to the economic interaction on a micro-regional, Scandinavian, and European scale. The discussed economic niches either in resource availability, production reputation, or other comparative advantages (Earle et al., 2015) would have secured the functionality of the local trade system. The tight knit cultural, ideological, and cosmological networks indicate that journeys within the NordicBA cultural sphere were much more common than with the rest of Europe despite the equal need for long-distance journeys.

5 Conflict and Alliances in the Nordic Bronze Age Economy

Exchange distributes raw materials, finished products, and services. Today, such interactions are conducted as trade which uses money as a value equivalent (Davies, 2016), but other forms of exchange have long existed. The existence of a generalized value equivalent in the European Bronze Age is in doubt, and nonmonetized gift exchanges and barter including bulk goods seem more fitting modes of exchange. Gift exchange has been discussed in archaeology (most recently Hansen, 2022), relying on the anthropological works of Marcel Mauss (2010) and Maurice Godelier (1999). Barter and trade were rarely separated for methodological problems (Sherratt, 1993). Thus, the term trade glosses over the range of possible exchange actions (Podėnas and Čivilytė, 2019). In his discussion of the topic, Colin Renfrew (1975) was concerned with the paths that goods could have traveled, and the intermitted agents involved. He identified ten modes of material flows but never considered violent means as a mode of transfer.

The fact that exotic foreign objects or imported raw materials ended up far away from their sources does not inform us about how they were transferred (Olausson, 1988). Warfare through raiding and looting can dislocate materials, objects, and humans, but these practices have been ignored because they were seen as the antithesis to trade (Polanyi et al., 1957; Polanyi, 2001; Renfrew, 1975). However, this does not seem to square with the overwhelming presence and social position of warriors during the NordicBA. Recently, the role of warriors and warfare in the NordicBA economy has been readdressed by detailing the pervading impact of warfare on social structure, ideology, beliefs, and the economy (Horn, 2018b; Lemonnier, 1991; Kristiansen, 2018; Kristiansen and Suchowska-Ducke, 2015).

A diversity of agents and institutions were involved in exchange, including traders, raiders (Horn and Kristiansen, 2018), secret societies connected to boatbuilding, and guilds (Ling et al., 2022), but also guest-friendship rules (*xenia*) (Kaul, 2017). Leaders likely established alliances, like political confederacies between micro-regional polities to enable cooperation in long-distance exchange (Ling et al., 2018a). Confederacies were hierarchical formations of decentralized complexity (Kradin, 2015) that linked polities with different interests. Institutions such as confederacies, guest-friendship, and other forms of alliances allowed for safe passages, resting, and resupply, thereby reducing risks which made journeys more calculable. Since confederacies often followed trade routes, they tend to take on a linear form, which was also observed for the NordicBA (Earle, 2017). Conflict and alliances had a profound impact on past economies. Therefore, it is important to consider both in the following to provide a fuller understanding of NordicBA economies.

5.1 The Role of Violence in the Economy

Trygve Haavelmo (1956) challenged the focus of economic theory on win–win situations and the presumed opposition of conflict and trade. He included appropriation in economic development, which became an increasingly important part of economic studies (Garfinkel and Skaperdas, 2007). Local NordicBA communities pursued at times shared interests through mutual economic interdependence which made them engage in peaceful exchange. However, without state regulation, no written legal systems framed economic and political relationships. Instead, negotiated networks of power existed that have been defined as anarchic (Hirshleifer, 1995). This fits well with interpretations of the NordicBA as complex decentralized chiefdoms (Earle, 2002; Kristiansen, 2010). Interpersonal and customary rules regulated intergroup contact, but these were difficult to enforce. Such networks of power were instable allowing for both cooperation and violence. Ethnographic examples show simultaneous patterns of exchange and conflicts between polities. Local groups of the Chumash of southern California accessed and exchanged many localized resources, including asphaltum, acorns, steatite, and obsidian that each local group desired (Fauvelle, 2013), but at the same time, intergroup violence also existed (Gamble, 2008).

Jack Hirshleifer (1995) accounted for factors disturbing balanced competition and leading to violence. He postulated that imbalances of strategic position could allow groups to accumulate comparative advantages leaving others without the means to engage in peaceful exchange. This and other factors like superior fighting power, advantages in population, complex constellations with more than two actors, and so on can lead to conflict, but also to larger, unstable group formations. Hirshleifer demonstrated that conflict and violence are not separated from economic practices; for example, raids could have rebalanced asymmetrical strategic positions. Among the Turkana in northwestern Kenya, group raiding redressed economic inequalities by redistributing resource–population imbalances (Hendrickson et al., 1998). Such processes were conceptualized by Sahlins (1965) as "negative reciprocity," that is, "receiving without giving" (Gouldner, 1960). Crucially, negative reciprocity causes the same distribution maps as peaceful exchange. For example, raided copper ore would have the same trace elements and lead isotopic patterns as traded ore. Unequal distribution of resources also means that local communities had reason to defend their comparative advantage because otherwise they risked losing participation in exchange networks.

5.2 Economic Imbalances during the Nordic Bronze Age: Limfjord

The high-profile resources during the NordicBA were amber, copper, tin, and possibly hides and slaves. Flint remained an important material throughout the NordicBA (Varberg, 2005; Goldhammer, 2015). Additionally, wool became increasingly important (Sabatini and Bergerbrant, 2020). Natural deposits of raw materials are unequally distributed, and some areas were in geographically more favorable positions to participate in metal or wool exchange networks. This afforded economic advantages to some micro-regions while disadvantaging others. Especially the Limfjord and its adjacent territories (Figure 11) stand out with their considerable coastal amber (Dahlström and Brost, 1996; Earle et al., 2022; Olsen and Earle, 2018) and flint sources. Flint was mined here and used to produce iconic flint daggers and arrowheads that were distributed throughout the Nordic sphere, Finland, Poland, and the Netherlands (Apel, 2001). Another possibility was the advantageous production of cattle hides seen in the EBA house 6 in Bjerre (Olsen and Earle, 2018).

The Limfjord was a 180-km-long passage during the Bronze Age connecting the North Sea and Kattegat in the north of Jutland because sea levels were c. 5 m higher than today (Andersen, 1990). Additionally, the calmer water made traveling faster and safer. This made it a meeting place for incoming and outgoing expeditions from the North Sea and the Atlantic Facade on one side and from the Baltic Sea on the other. Thus, apart from being favored by natural resources, Limfjord communities were strategically placed to control trade and launch trading/raiding expeditions. This provided excellent opportunities to gain power over local, regional, and long-distance exchanges making these groups gatekeepers for incoming ore and other goods (Figure 11).

Some important material shortages existed also in the Limfjord that would have encouraged local groups to exchange goods with contemporaries in other Nordic areas. Dramatic deforestation since the arrival of the Neolithic FBC went on during the NordicBA, causing timber shortages. The ongoing destruction of grazing land in favor of monumental barrow construction that stripped turfs may have damaged livelihood (Holst et al., 2013). Both opened economic opportunities for some communities to supply these needs. However, it seems unlikely that all communities could capitalize, which left some disadvantaged,

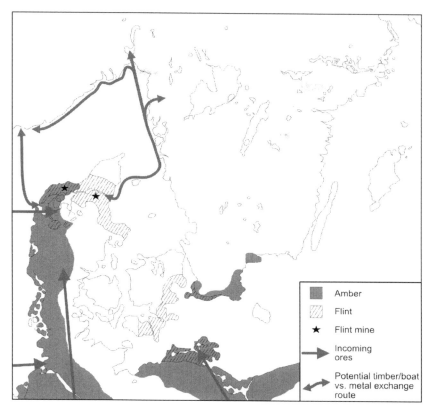

Figure 11 Example of imbalances in the distribution of natural resources and geographical position during the NordicBA on the example of the Limfjord region. Also illustrated is the potential for interregional exchange relationships (after Dahlström & Brost, 1996; Varberg 2005; drawn by Christian Horn)

creating economic imbalances. In line with Hirshleifer's theory, raids could have provided essential resources to such deprived communities (Horn, 2018b; Ling et al., 2018b).

5.3 Evidence for Violence

If economic imbalances were redressed through violence during the NordicBA, traces should be expected in the archaeological record. Ample evidence for warfare and violence exists in the NordicBA. Several hillforts have been ^{14}C-dated to the NordicBA and some fortified settlements existed, which clearly indicate = a need for defensive and protective installations. These were mostly situated along important sea routes, protecting central settlements like Apalle in East Middle Sweden, the Håga complex, and

Hallunda in Mälardalen (Artursson et al., 2017; Wehlin, 2013). Along a ford in the Tollense valley (Northern Germany), remains of a large battle (1300–1200 BCE) have been discovered that probably engaged many combatants on each side with over 100 killed (Jantzen et al., 2011, 2014). This was shortly before the cultural transition to the LBA when cremation became prevalent and burial wealth decreased dramatically. Isotopic analyses of individuals from this battlefield showed that some casualties were nonlocals coming from South-Central Europe (Price et al., 2019). Thus, this battle can be interpreted as linked to the rising Central European Urnfield culture which brought upheaval and unrest.

Examples of smaller violent encounters include remains of twenty-two massacred children, women, and men buried in Sund (Norway). In addition to violent trauma, indications of life-long hard labor and malnutrition suggest that they belonged to an exploited class, that is, slaves (Fyllingen, 2003, 2006). Another mass killing occurred earlier, during the LN–EBA transition, in Sømme (Norway). A cairn contained remains of at least six cremated individuals including an infant, of which four were hanged (Denham et al., 2018; Høgestøl, 2003). Other victims of violence have been uncovered in Granhammar (Sweden; Lindström, 2009), Kråkerøy (Norway; Holck, 1987), and Over Vindinge (Denmark; Kjær, 1912). In instances where the killer's weapon is known, it appears to have been of local origin, including the Nordic spearhead embedded in the pelvis of the deceased from Over Vindinge. The man in Granhammar, who, according to isotope analysis, traveled c. 500 km to his killing place from Scania, was probably attacked with a local ax type.

Substantial precious bronze was invested in weaponry even ignoring bronze arrowheads that have come to new prominence through the discoveries in the Tollense valley (Section 4.2.1). Studies of use-wear on EBA swords, spears, and daggers demonstrated abundant traces of use in combat (Figures 10(b)–(d) and 12(a)) (Bunnefeld, 2016; Horn, 2013; Horn and Karck, 2019; Kristiansen, 1984, 2002). Unfortunately, the study of LBA weapon use is absent for southern Scandinavia. The battlefield in the Tollense valley can serve as an example that evidence for prehistoric violence is an "iceberg phenomenon." This means that we observe only the tip of the iceberg, that is, a small subset of weapons and victims, while the bulk remains hidden from view. Every individual discovered in the Tollense valley was a victim of violence, but only 7 percent show battle-related skeletal trauma, and some were old, healed wounds (Brinker et al., 2014; Brinker et al., 2016). The vast majority of weaponry known from the NordicBA was discovered in ritual contexts, which means that we can only observe them when customs stipulated a weapon sacrifice or that they should accompany a deceased.

Additionally, Scandinavian rock art has more depictions of warriors, combat, local weapon types, and other violence than any other Bronze Age region in Europe (Figure 12) (Horn, 2023; Ling and Cornell 2017). This evidence clearly demonstrates that violence like raiding was common between NordicBA and perhaps other European communities, while larger-scale escalations were also possible (Horn, 2023).

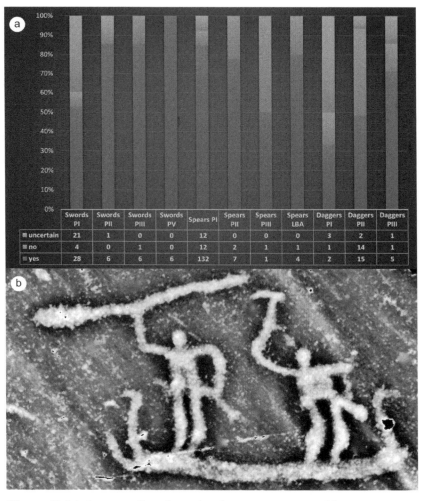

	Swords PI	Swords PII	Swords PIII	Swords PV	Spears PI	Spears PII	Spears PIII	Spears LBA	Daggers PI	Daggers PII	Daggers PIII
uncertain	21	1	0	0	12	0	0	0	3	2	1
no	4	0	1	0	12	2	1	1	1	14	1
yes	28	6	6	6	132	7	1	4	2	15	5

Figure 12 (a) Amount of combat-related use-wear separated by weapon type and chronology (after Horn 2013; Horn and Karck, 2019); (b) two maritime warriors in Bro Utmark (Tanum 192:1), Sweden (laser scan by Ellen Meijer, visualization https://tvt.dh.gu.se/)

5.4 Raiding, Slaving, and Trading

Raiding was probably the major mode of warfare during the NordicBA (Horn, 2016, 2023) equalizing economic imbalances and seizing wealth. This was likely an opportunistic strategy that can be compared to the much later raiding and trading of Vikings (Catling, 2010). This comparison also indicates that raiding was used strategically in power struggles as part of the political economy (Zilmer, 2006). We can theorize that raiding/trading expeditions caused labor shortages because voyagers left the agropastoral sector to engage in these activities. Some shortages in labor could have been alleviated through alliances; however, where this was not possible, slave-taking raids may have provided farm labor (Ling et al., 2018b; Mikkelsen, 2020). While elusive, some evidence of slaves has been suggested for the NordicBA including housing arrangements (Mikkelsen, 2020), hostage or slave images in rock art, that is, Leirfall (Norway), Ekenberg, and Aspeberget (Sweden) (Figure 13), burials in simple, flat inhumation graves

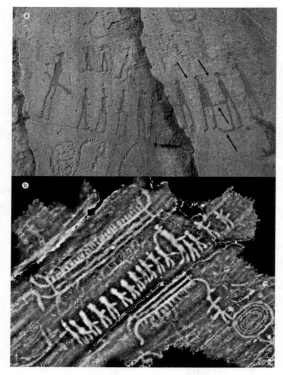

Figure 13 Rock art showing potential slaving scenes: (a) Leirfall (field III), Trøndelag, Norway (photo by Arve Kjersem, 2017); (b) Ekenberg (Östra Eneby 23:1), Norrköping, Sweden (laser scan by Ellen Meijer, visualization https://tvt.dh.gu.se/)

(Bergerbrant et al., 2017), and the massacre in Sund (Fyllingen, 2003). Slaves themselves may have become a commodity, in which some communities specialized, allowing them to engage in local and European trade by moving slaves to areas where they were highly desired (Ling et al., 2018b). Neil Price (2016) summarized the parallel Viking case with the phrase "raiding is slaving is trading." Overall, the evidence indicates that slavery could have been an integrated part of NordicBA economy.

5.5 Alliances

The suggestion that seafaring raiding expeditions required the cooperation of several farmsteads in alliances will be illustrated on the Torsted hoard in the following. By accepting the population estimates to calculate bronze availability for each farmstead, we arrived at an average of 100–150 g per year (Section 4.2.1). However, assuming that wealthier farms probably had more bronze available, then we can suggest that they had about 1–2 kg of bronze available per year. A newly produced spearhead may have weighed c. 150–200 g on average and an ax c. 200–250 g, which means the Torsted hoard would have consumed between 7.4 and 9.75 kg of bronze. This would have depleted four to nine years' worth of bronze supply for a single farmstead. Thus, to enable production without making a farm susceptible to shortages, several farms could have collaborated. Following this thought, four to nine wealthy farms could have given up their yearly supply of bronze, and eight to eighteen farms could have been involved if they gave up half that amount. It means that an estimated total of more than 40–270 people may have cooperated.

The limited combat marks on the Torsted spears suggest that they have been used only a few times (Horn, 2013). Thus, these weapons may have outfitted a warband of maybe forty-seven warriors on a couple of raids. Some higher-ranking crew may have had swords that, for some reason, were not sacrificed. Perhaps we can assume that weapons had been produced to outfit a party of fifty people. Evidence from rock art demonstrates that swords, spears, and axes accompanied boat crews on their journeys and considering that Torsted is only about a day's march from the shore, it is reasonable that the weapons represent several boat crews. Rock art informs us that the average number of crew sitting in pairs was twelve to fourteen individuals per boat (Ling, 2014). Thus, the weapons in the Torsted hoard plus the theoretical three swords could have armed three to four boat crews if all members had a weapon.

If only four farmsteads supplied the metal for the weaponry, then all or most members of the farms would have had to join the boat crews. This fact, and that they potentially gave up an entire year of bronze supply, makes this scenario unlikely. Should eighteen farmsteads have collaborated, then only two to three members each would have had to leave. While we cannot give any specific numbers, the most likely scenario can be assumed to be within this span. This model demonstrates that NordicBA communities probably formed alliances to outfit and conduct expeditions while keeping their economies viable.

5.6 Conclusion

Uneven distribution of resources and geographical conditions created regional economic imbalances in the NordicBA. Material culture, ideology, and victims of violence demonstrate frequent raiding in power struggles, to redress economic imbalances, and for slave-taking to supply labor and for economic gains. Farmsteads formed alliances to outfit and crew trading and raiding parties. Depending on the circumstance, the number of involved individuals in such an alliance may have exceeded 250, making such alliances not only an economic factor but also leading to the organization of larger polities. These alliances probably included often and rapidly changing constellations including the cooperation of inland and coastal communities. Some of these collaborations could also have been exclusively inland communities, for example, along rivers or lakes. Larger confederacies may have formed along seaways; however, they were probably unstable, never leading to permanent political structures.

6 Bronze Age Political Formations: Micro-regional Case Studies

Despite its outward uniformity, the NordicBA contained different local polities based on various organizational strategies. To illustrate, this section will point to different micro-regions with contrasting organizational strategies and discuss how they could have formed alliances because they were essential to maintain and improve the local economies. The Limfjord in northern Jutland, Jæren in southwest Norway, the inner-fjord district of Sogn, and Tanum in western Sweden provide ideal case studies to define the space local polities occupied, and the landscape they exploited.

6.1 Limfjord

In the Limfjord, the subsistence economy was based on individual farmsteads with a high degree of self-sufficiency forming the basic element in the land-based agropastoral sector (Bech et al., 2018; Earle et al., 2015; Kristiansen, 2000). Farmstead density was 1 per km^2 and even higher in some areas (Bech et al., 2018). Two major elements dominated subsistence production: cattle breeding and agriculture. While cattle breeding was a major economic component since pastoral Corded Ware groups (c. 2800 BCE) immigrated to

Scandinavia (Kristiansen, 2000), agriculture increased in importance with the beginning of the NordicBA. Archaeobotanical evidence indicates that agricultural production was augmented by focusing on different crops to maximize output (Kristiansen et al., 2020: section 3.5) and developing a more predictive, expansive, and stable economy (Iversen, 2017). Central to each farmstead were three-aisle residences c. 18 m on average in length with wattle-and-daub walls (Bech et al., 2018). A few longhouses were over 30-m long with massive roof-supporting posts and planked walls, comparable to later Viking Age halls (Artursson, 2015). Such halls were attributed to chieftains that funded their construction and that of associated large barrows; free farmers, servants, and slaves carried out labor on an obligatory basis (Earle, 2019).

Estimates predict that each ordinary farmstead produced about 60–80 percent of its food, and about 50–60 percent of its technology (pottery, stone tools such as flint sickles, and stone hammers). The foodstuff consisted of 80–90 percent agropastoral products supplemented by fish and wild game (Bech et al., 2018: section 3). Chiefly farmsteads showed an even higher degree of self-sufficiency with an estimated 90–100 percent production of their own food and 80–100 percent of their technology. This means chiefly farms could have worked as coordinating nodes for local communities that organized local and regional production, exchange, and distribution of complex technology.

A specific form of flint dagger was produced in Jutland during the LN and NordicBA Period I (Figures 9(c) and 11) that became widely distributed in Scandinavia and beyond, including eighty specimens recorded in Tanum (Ling, 2014). Concentrated cattle raising and hide-making may have been for export (Earle et al., 1998). Amber was collected at a larger scale perhaps to access metal and other prestige goods (Earle, Bech and Villa, 2023). Bronze axes, for example, presumably supplied local demands, whereas swords and other prestigious objects may have been for regional trade (Melheim et al., 2018). Elite farmsteads seem to have controlled distribution and funded or managed weapon production, boatbuilding, and crewing of boats. Such families could have organized alliances through dependencies perhaps temporally coalescing into larger confederacies, which would in turn yield greater gains for these elites (Section 6.5). Overall, the evidence suggests a top-down distribution of resources and perhaps (the threat of) violence as coercive measures to secure social cohesion within larger chiefdoms.

6.2 Jæren

Jæren contains low-lying sandy plains, moraines, smaller rivers, lakes, and wetlands (Figure 1). Along its coast are dangerous sea crossings but also protective small islands. Further inland exist ample upland resources and grazing opportunities (Prøsch-Danielsen et al., 2020), and beyond, mountainous areas for hunting. An important feature is its potential for maritime trade combined with well-drained soil suitable for farming. This micro-region was exploited already during the LN, and archaeology points to innovations, like cereal cultivation, animal husbandry, and permanent two-aisled longhouses, at this time (Børsheim, 2005). A noticeable increase in the pollen record of ribwort (*Plantago lanceolate*) indicates pastoralism, deforestation, and expanding heathland continuing throughout the NordicBA along the coast (Prøsch-Danielsen, 1993; Prøsch-Danielsen and Simonsen, 2000). The climate had warm summers, frequent rainfalls, and mild winters creating a vegetation zone that allowed for a longer growing season and the possibility to keep livestock outside year-round (Moen et al., 1999). Bronze Age pollen analyses indicated cereal cultivation and increasing open grazing land; cereal macro remains and bones from domesticated animals supported this conclusion (Høgestøl and Prøsch-Danielsen, 2006; Prøsch-Danielsen and Simonsen, 2000; Prøsch- Danielsen and Soltvedt, 2012; Soltvedt, 2007).

Jæren is distinguished from other areas in Norway by frequent barrows that emerged around 1500 BCE. They have been suggested to assert property relationships based on ancestry and were found throughout the area often situated on hills and promontories overlooking the coastline (e.g., Myhre 1981). Around 175 burials date to the LN–NordicBA of the county Rogaland, which Jæren dominates (Austvoll, 2019; Larsen, 1997; Myhre, 2004) representing the richest record of NordicBA barrows and material culture in Norway. Most barrows were constructed between 1500 and 1100 BCE, indicating an intensive phase of social consolidation with a political economy of elite management and trade (Austvoll, 2020). They were built with earth and turf, sometimes surrounded by curb stones, and containing a stone burial cist (Austvoll, 2019; Myhre, 2004). Additionally, stone cairns without earthen mantles were common along the Scandinavian coastline. Some burials closely resembled their South Scandinavian counterparts in size and burial goods. The Rege mound (Figure 14(a) and (b)), for example, measured 20 m in diameter and 3 m in height. Its monumentality was accentuated by its position on a large hill overlooking the coast and inland. One of its two stone cists had a rich Period II assemblage that included a bronze dagger, neck plate, belt plate, spiral-ended fibula, two arm-rings, and smaller hair adornments (Oma, 2020). Pieces of bronze tubes may indicate a corded skirt like the famous Egtved oak burial in Jutland (Felding, 2016). One stone slab at the head of the cist was decorated with concentric circles and cup marks. Carved grave slabs were uncommon but appear to cluster in a few micro-regions during the NordicBA (Figure 14(b)–(e)). The most famous is

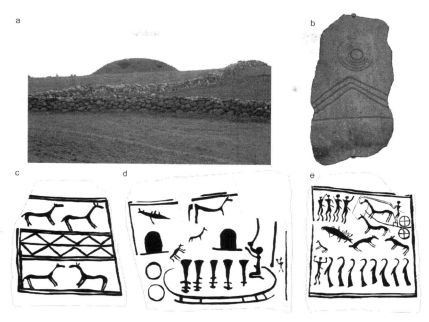

Figure 14 (a) The barrow in Rege, Sola, Norway in the landscape; (b) carved slab from the stone cist in the barrow in Rege (photos a and b: by Museum of Archaeology, University of Stavanger, CC-BY-NC-ND); (c)–(e) Carved slabs of the stone cist in the Bredarör cairn in Kivik, Simrishamn, Sweden (laser scan by Ellen Meijer, visualization https://tvt.dh.gu.se/; interpretation by Christian Horn)

the large Kivik cairn in southeastern Scania with richly decorated stone slabs forming its cist (Figure 14(c)–(e); Goldhahn, 2006; Syvertsen, 2005).

The Rege barrow was among several burials with a typical female artifact assembly. In Period II, female graves outnumbered male graves; however, in Period III, male burials dominated, relocating toward the northern part of the micro-region (Myhre, 2004). At Sothaug on the Tananger Peninsula, the barrow had a similar placement on a hilltop with a good view over the surrounding landscape. At 40 m in diameter and a height of 5–6 m, it was significantly larger than others (Myhre, 1980). In 1842, a farmer uncovered a stone cist that contained human bones, a bronze sword, two bronze buttons, and woolen cloth (Myhre, 1981).

The pattern of monumental barrows suggests social stratification with access to exotic goods. Metalworking sites elsewhere (Melheim et al., 2016; Sörman, 2017, 2018) documented local production of some metal objects. In addition to the strategic maritime placement controlling communication and trade, marriage alliances may have been another factor for the area's success.

The transition from two-aisled houses occurred around 1600 BCE (Fyllingen, 2015), and a few three-aisled longhouses could equal barrows in monumentality (Eriksen and Austvoll, 2020). Most longhouses were intermediate in size averaging 17.6 × 6.3 m (Austvoll, 2021). The largest grouping of houses was near Orre Lake, which could have been a strategic harbor (Austvoll, 2019). Several hamlets are known, for example, from Tjora, Mykleburst, and Forsandmoen suggesting a micro-regional hierarchical settlement structure (Dahl, 2014; Fyllingen, 2012; Løken, 2021). While most houses had wattle-and-daub walls, some with thicker posts could have had plank-built (bole) walls like those in south Scandinavia (Austvoll, 2021). Subsistence was based on crop cultivation documented by charred cereal grains (naked barley and emmer) and quern stones (Løken, 1987; Prøsch-Danielsen and Soltvedt, 2012). Traces of animal husbandry are limited, but sheep have been documented (Oma, 2018). Domestic artifacts included ceramic sherds and flint objects and debris (Austvoll, 2021).

The rich material record in Jæren indicates a substantial population relative to other areas in northwestern Scandinavia. Chiefs likely had strategic control over seaways and bottlenecks along the coast, gaining power over travel, exchange, and warfare for the accumulation of metal wealth. They may have invested in labor force and material for barrows and house constructions; however, individual farms likely preserved a sense of autonomy (Earle, 2021). The political hierarchy likely lay in maritime control and trade rather than staple finance of cereal cultivation and animal husbandry (Prescott et al., 2018).

6.3 Inner Sogn

Inner Sogn is a stark contrast to Jæren and the Limfjord because it is situated at the end of a long fjord, 170 km removed from coastal sea routes, with alpine mountains, small patches of arable land in estuaries. The population density was lower than in the core areas and spread across this vast and fragmented area. Multiple vegetation zones exist, but most settlements were in the southern boreal zone (Moen et al., 1999). The micro-region has rich soils for farming in low-lying areas (Austad et al., 1991).

Settlement excavations documented cereal cultivation and animal husbandry as key subsistence resources (Halvorsen, 2005, 2006, 2008; Hjelle, 2003). Layers of charcoal-bearing earth (Olsen, 2009) may document forest clearance, and the presence of *Plantago lanceolata* indicates pastures (Hjelle, 2003, 2005). The Skrivarhelleren rock shelter produced indirect evidence of wool-based production, with caprine bones and bone objects like pins and needles (Prescott and Melheim, 2017). What made this area successful is the availability of marine resources in the fjord near individual farmsteads and cereal cultivation in lower lands, combined with ample economic opportunities including extensive seasonal pastures in the subalpine areas, freshwater fishing, lithic procurement, and hunting (Prescott, 1991a, 1995). While NordicBA cairns were situated close to seaways along the mouth of the fjord, monumental barrows and chiefly longhouses were absent. Thus, there was a strong economic emphasis on self-sufficiency and bottom-up cooperation between households (Austvoll, 2021).

Initially, no longhouses were longer than 15 m with about 10 m length on average (Austvoll, 2021). Some irregular three-aisled longhouses are known, 14 C-dated to the LN/EBA (Diinhoff, 2005; Olsen, 2013), but two-aisled longhouses dominate in the archaeological record (Diinhoff, 2013). Several longhouses with large postholes or trenches might have had plank-built walls, likely reflecting the area's rich timber resources.

Metal objects, often of an early date, have been discovered as stray finds or at settlement sites (Anfinset, 2015). Two flanged axes and a bracelet dated to Period I were discovered in loose gravel in Veim in Aurland (Anfinset, 2015). Another three flanged axes and a riveted metal dagger represent contemporaneous stray finds. Apart from Bronze Age metalwork, the Skrivarhelleren rock shelter provided evidence of metal production already during the LN (Prescott, 1991a, 1995). Lithic finds, like imported flint daggers and simple shaft-hole axes correspond well with the metalwork patterns, perhaps indicative of a micro-region that was well integrated into wider trade networks (Hjelle et al., 2006).

Overall, instead of being organized by top-down coercion, like in Limfjord or Jæren, local communities gained a strategic advantage by organizing households cooperatively. Cooperative communities operated differently compared to coercive polities along the coastal zones. Transport by boat along the fjord allowed easy communication and connected settlements and production in different fjord branches. The flint and metalwork demonstrate that these communities were able to engage in wider exchange networks, participating and positioning themselves in a political economy. Access to mountain resources could have facilitated wool-based production (Prescott and Melheim, 2017) and frozen wild game finds documented hunting perhaps for fur, pelts, and antlers (Callanan, 2014; Nesje et al., 2012). Both could have provided products to create comparative advantages through specialization which would have given bottom-up opportunities to cooperatively organized households to participate in regional and long-distance exchange networks.

6.4 Tanum

Tanum is situated in northern Bohuslän at the Skagerrak coast north of the Kattegat strait in the nemoral and boreonemoral vegetation border zone (Moen et al., 1999). Tanum is remarkable because it has the highest concentration of Bronze Age rock art in Europe. The rock art was located in c. 70 percent of all cases near large, shallow bays and boats (c. 2000) are the dominant image (Figure 15(a)–(d)). Other figurative images depict warriors, weapons, animals, cup marks, and more. The spatial distribution of the rock art appears to document a ritual chain of boatbuilding from higher ground, where trees were

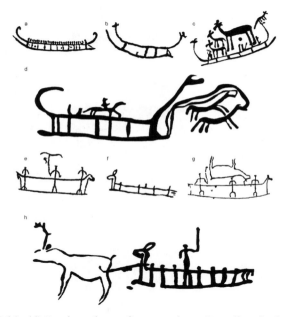

Figure 15 (a)–(d) Rock art boats from southern Scandinavia dating to the NordicBA and (e)–(h) similar boats made by hunter-gatherers in Alta, Norway: (a) typical EBA boat with crew strokes and division of the hull; (b) boat with horse-headed prows; (c) boat-carrying animals (horses?) with heads very similar to the prows of the boat; (d) horse-headed boat towed by a horse team with a horseback rider on board that may be a later addition; (e) crew holding a T-shaped implement; (f) crew indicated as strokes and divisions of the hull depicted; (g) boat with crew carrying a hunted elk, the same animal species that may have provided hide for constructing the boat; (h) elk-headed boat towed by an elk; interpretations by Christian Horn based on documentation by the Alta Museum Rock Art Archive (a–d: http://altarockart.no/fotoweb/) and laser scan by Ellen Meijer visualized with https://tvt.dh.gu.se/ (e–h)

cut for the craft, to rock art adjacent to settlements where crafts were roughed out, and, finally, at launching sites for departure and return (Goldhahn and Ling, 2013; Ling et al., 2021).

The communities here lacked some prerequisites to produce a wealth-financed economy that was present in the Limfjord and Jæren micro-regions. Instead, they engaged in a more diversified economy composed of agropastoralism supplemented by fishing, hunting, and timber extraction (Ling et al., 2018b). Farmsteads produced perhaps about 60–80 percent of their foodstuff and about 30–50 percent of their technology. Nutrition consisted of 60–80 percent of agropastoral products with fish and wild game supplementing the remaining needs (Ling, 2014). The importance of marine resources for local household self-sufficiency was demonstrated by cultural layers containing fish bones, fishing hooks, and fishing scenes on rock art (Ling, 2014). The importance of boats for these communities was probably as distinctive as seen in the Haida culture, northwestern USA, where such vessels served for fishing, hunting, trade, warfare, and long-distance exchange (Ling et al., 2021), making it likely that a significant number of households were involved in and depended upon boatbuilding.

The coast, however, was deforested perhaps already by 1600 BCE (Ling et al., 2018b). Local communities in Tanum could have compensated for this shortage by exploiting timber sources further inland which they were potentially familiar with through long traditions of working with lumber and boatbuilding. Evidence for this may be rock art with shared imagery along rivers, fjords, and lakes penetrating deep into the Swedish hinterlands (Nimura et al., 2020). Additionally, statistical analysis shows a correlation between tools for boatbuilding and sites with rock art boats near ancient seaways (Ling, 2014). Other more concrete evidence of shipbuilding could include seaside fire-cracked stone-filled pits containing wood species used to construct prehistoric boats (Petersson, 2009). Ethnographic studies document the use of fire-heated stones and water to steam wood in traditional watercraft production, particularly for the keel and the side portions (Ling et al., 2021). This may have helped households in Tanum to establish comparative advantages in timber and boat production which was supported by its relative proximity to the Limfjord, the Oslofjord, Western Norway, and across inland water bodies to East Sweden.

Boatbuilding requires collective work in production and in logistics to fell and transport appropriately large trees from remote areas. Experimental archaeology has shown that c. 20-m-long Bronze Age plank-built canoes needed about 6500 h in construction (Ling et al., 2018b). Chiefs could have funded such work, for example, by supplying nutrition or materials for tools to establish ownership of the boats. However, Tanum is a low-density population area without chiefly longhouses. With an average length of c. 12–15 m, longhouses were only marginally bigger than in Inner Sogn. Despite this, large cairns, precious bronzes, and rich rock art panels strongly indicate regional and trans-regional exchange and the presence of elites. Although Tanum lacks important natural resources like flint and amber, flint sickles, scrapers, and daggers were very frequent tools at local farmsteads. In addition, copper and tin had to be acquired from outside, which means communities in Tanum had not only the incentive to organize expeditions to gain these resources but evidently did so very successfully. Together with the pervasive maritime warrior representations in rock art, this could indicate that it was home to larger contingents of the trader-raiders of the NordicBA (Horn, 2023; Ling and Cornell, 2017). Tanum seems to have features of cooperative and coercive community organization which may have an explanation in its closeness to local elites in the Limfjord micro-region.

6.5 Economic Complementarity between Tanum and Limfjord

The micro-regional case studies suggest interaction between the land-based communities of the Limfjord with sea-based communities in Tanum as indicated by flint daggers and bronzes recovered in the region (Sections 6.2 and 6.4). The high frequency of metalwork in the Limfjord and matching lead isotope signals with metalwork throughout Scandinavia indicated that this was potentially the major hub for the redistribution of metal during the EBA. If raiding was not the sole factor in the distribution of this material, then it is possible that chiefly households in Limfjord accounted for their needs by establishing timber or boat trade with communities, for example, in Tanum. For communities in Tanum, transferring a large labor force from agricultural to the maritime sector may lead to imbalances in the domestic production that could be supplemented by chiefs from the Limfjord. This could have been achieved by supporting boatbuilding with food, materials, and slaves (Figure 11). Such assistance could have come through competitive feasting with lavish gift exchanges to exert power and control over cooperatively organized families (Ling et al., 2018b). The driving factor was perhaps that Jutland was largely deforested by 1500 BCE increasing the demand for timber and external boat production. This could have influenced communities in Limfjord to attempt to increase their agropastoral surplus. Interestingly, historical comparisons dated to the twelfth century AD show that northern Bohuslän exchanged timber and boats with Jutland for agropastoral products (Ling et al., 2018b).

Similar reciprocal relationships may have linked the NordicBA sphere at different distances and in different combinations of exchanged goods and modes of exchange, always with the potential for violence. Such systems would have been inherently unstable because of the economic interdependence between micro-regions that diminished the self-sufficiency of their economies; however, it would have served a political economy based on flows of wealth between regions which created an ever-changing network of differently organized communities, interdependence, support, and alliances, but also of adversaries. Constant high mobility with frequently shifting contacts between partners and competitors may have given rise to the uniformity of the NordicBA archaeological record.

All case studies document the attempt of local farmsteads to be self-sufficient, but the technologies and economies of micro-regions became interdependent, partially because the NordicBA economy was highly dependent on metal flows from the outside. Environmental benefits, freedom of mobility, resource ownership, and transportation technology are all important factors in determining comparative advantages between micro-regions and to the expanding European trade economy more generally. The outcome was a strong engagement with the broader European world.

7 Encountering Europe

The previous discussion implies that NordicBA polities depended on contacts with regions elsewhere in Europe, especially to acquire copper, tin, gold, and perhaps salt (Sections 4). We believe that foodstuffs and commodities surplus produced by the local domestic economy supplied maritime expeditions and material for exchange of either bulk goods or gifts, or to produce weaponry for raids (Sections 3–5). Furthermore, we have reviewed evidence that maritime expeditions were undertaken by allied groups rather than individual actors (Section 5.5). While the indirect evidence is plentiful, direct evidence for the encounters of Nordic and other European communities and how they traveled to meet each other is surprisingly rare. We discuss the available evidence for encounters and possible means of transport next, because boats and boat journeys were such crucial elements of the NordicBA society and economy.

7.1 Scandinavians Going Abroad, and How to Recognize Them

Advances in radiocarbon dating, lead, strontium and oxygen isotopes, and ancient DNA allow for new interpretations of the sources of metal ores and the movements of humans. Despite significant challenges, the potential to study migration, traders, and slaves is intriguing as illustrated by the findings at Cliffs End Farm on Thanet

(McKinley et al., 2014). Thanet provided evidence for the meeting of individuals from Scandinavia with other Europeans highlighting its importance as a node in European exchange networks. Skeletal material of thirty-one individuals was retrieved dating to the British LBA and Early Iron Age; a phase that was contemporary with the NordicBA. According to isotope data, three individuals may have grown up in "Scandinavian" climatic conditions, which could mean that they traveled from Scandinavia to Cliffs End. All were found in or near one feature that also contained the bones of two individuals from Southern European regions, that is, the Mediterranean or Iberia and four locals (McKinley et al., 2014).

Cliffs End also demonstrated that encounters between such distant European communities were complex, potentially involving violence. The skeleton of a male, possibly of Scandinavian origin, was discovered tightly packed, suggesting that he may have arrived dead and stuffed into a bag in a semidecomposed state. Furthermore, among six individuals with trauma, three were weapon-related injuries. An elderly local woman was killed by blows with a sharp implement against the back of her head. The origin of the other two victims is unclear; one died from a stab wound to the lungs, and a 10–14-year-old had been beaten to death with a blunt implement (McKinley et al., 2014). Others may have died through violence that left no traces on their bones like on the battlefield in the Tollense valley (Brinker et al., 2014: section 5.4).

Located at the eastern entry into the British Channel, Cliffs End controlled a crucial nexus for travelers along the Atlantic facade. People gathering here from distant places could have exchanged amber, salt, copper, and tin. Material evidence for such contacts between Scandinavians and Iberian communities may come from an Iberian looped palstave discovered at Lake Tåkern, Eastern Middle Sweden. Conversations that ensued during these encounters may have had long-term effects, visible in rock art motifs shared between Iberia and Scandinavia with the depiction of horned warriors, specific hand gestures, chariots, and more (Díaz-Guardamino et al., 2022; Ling and Uhnér, 2014). However, depending on circumstances, such trade meetings may have gone awry, for example, through disagreements over exchanged quantities, procedural mistakes, or cultural misunderstandings. People caught up in hostilities were perhaps killed or injured, including the elderly woman who could have played an important role, for example, as mediator or expert in the proper, that is, customary conduct of such encounters.

7.2 Scandinavians on Tour: Plank-Built Boats and Alternatives

The geographical position of Cliffs End emphasized that maritime travel was the major mode of mobility between the Atlantic facade and Scandinavia during the NordicBA. Despite boat depictions in Scandinavian rock art with excellent evidence for their use, it is often repeated that evidence for waterborne vessels remains remarkably scant (Bradley, 2022; Ling, 2014). Spectacular discoveries of Bronze Age vessels like the Dover boat (Clark, 2004) are so far absent for the NordicBA. A long known find dated to 1400–1200 BCE from Alva Myr (Gotland), which was reused as a coffin, was possibly part of a vessel with hewn cleats (Floderus, 1931; Wehlin, 2013). The closest Scandinavian parallel is the Early Iron Age plank-built boat discovered in Hjortspring (Denmark) dating to c. 400–300 BCE (Crumlin- Pedersen and Trakadas, 2003; Randsborg, 1995). Archaeological experiments have demonstrated that it was a seaworthy vessel (Vinner, 2003; Figure 16).

Over 20,000 boats have been carved in Scandinavian bedrock surfaces and loose boulders (Bradley, 2022: figure 15). While a few depictions occur on

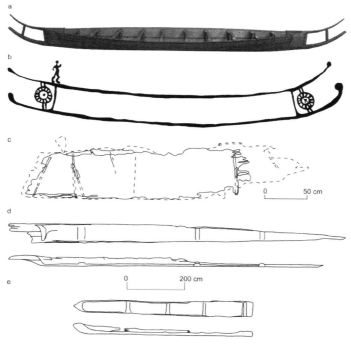

Figure 16 Boat finds: (a) Hjortspring, Als, Denmark (3D reconstruction by Rich Potter); (b) rock art boat from Litsleby (Tanum 75:1), Sweden (photogrammetry by Rich Potter visualized with https://tvt.dh.gu.se/); (c) Byslätt, Istorp, Sweden (after von Arbin and Lindberg, 2017); (d) Varpelev, East Zealand, Denmark; (e) Vestersø, Limfjord, Denmark (d–e: after Kastholm, 2015) (all drawings by Christian Horn)

boulders in Denmark, most of the boat engravings here are on bronze razors and knives in rich burials. One boat depiction has even survived on a piece of wood, which may indicate a wider tradition of making boat images on a larger variety of canvases such as wooden vessels or perhaps on house walls. This would represent a massive increase in scale for the use of boat images and would probably indicate an even greater importance for such vessels (Bengtsson, 2017). These images represent lived practices in an ideologically filtered representation of reality (Ling and Cornell, 2010). The plank-built boat from Hjortspring closely resembles rock art depictions and images on metalwork (Bradley, 2006; Kaul, 1998, 2003). Thus, this boat casts a late spotlight on a pervasive boat design tradition for seaworthy plank-built vessels that lasted at least 1400–1500 years.

Other vessels could also be depicted on the rocks. Skin boats are known from the northern rock art tradition of Scandinavia that began during the Mesolithic and lasted perhaps through the Bronze Age (Gjerde, 2010; Helskog, 1999). Such boats were created by spanning sewn animal hides over a frame usually made from wood and sealing the stitches with pitch, tar, or resin (Figure 15(e)–(h)). The rock art boats in the north, sometimes fitted with elk-head prows, indicate that elk skin may have been used. Similar technologies could have been in use during the NordicBA. Knud Valbjørn (2003) observed that some details of the Hjortspring boat could be remnants of an older Bronze Age skin boat tradition by building a scale model of this vessel as a skin boat. The argument is supported by the ribs that are shown in rock art which could be the observable wooden frame of boats over which the skins were tightly drawn. From 1300 BCE or perhaps somewhat earlier, the prows of the boats were decorated with horse heads. Analogous to the elk-head boats, this could be the species that provided hides to construct the vessels. An example of a Bronze Age skin boat (coracle) potentially made from horse skin has been discovered in Scotland where it was used as a coffin (Watkins, 1980). Additionally, ethnographic examples and historical sources support this possibility (Hornell, 2014). Horse hides would have been a highly valuable and prestigious resource which could have been a way to manifest power in the NordicBA political economy. It would be a resource that could have been produced by the domestic economy, that is, through breeding.

Instead of skin, bark could have been used to build the outer hull of boats. One of the few European finds of a bark boat comes from the bank of the river Viskan (Byslätt, Sweden; Figure 16(c)). New radiocarbon dating revealed that this canoe, traditionally seen as an Iron Age vessel, had a LBA date (Arbin and Lindberg, 2017). That means such vessels were used in Scandinavia at least since the beginning of Period V. A worked, slightly curved log discovered next to this boat could indicate an outrigger (Arbin and Lindberg, 2017). Such a constructional element stabilized the vessel to increase its seaworthiness. James Hornell (2014) mentions, for example, extensive use of single outriggers on the canoes of island-dwelling people of southeast Asia and Oceania.

Another type of vessel in use during the NordicBA were logboats (dugout canoes), which were made by digging out a log using axes, adzes, and fire setting, or by splitting a log which was then expanded using, for example, heated water (Figure 16(a) and (b)). Most Scandinavian logboats were unified by the presence of a platform in the aft, and sometimes also in the stem (Kastholm, 2015). This may have increased the stability and the structural integrity of the boat (Rogers, 2011). Only two logboats radiocarbon-dated to the NordicBA are known. One was discovered in Strö (Sweden, 1130–930 BCE) and the other in Varplev (Denmark, 1260–790 BCE). And additional five vessels either belonged to the LBA or the Earliest Iron Age. A logboat from the river Aller close to Gifhorn (Germany) was made from an oak felled in 1138 BCE (Eichfeld, 2020). There are another 107 logboats without proper scientific dating from the area, among which further Bronze Age boats may be discovered in the future.[1]

A large variety of boats provided transport for NordicBA communities and their emerging economic relationships at all levels – micro-regional, regional, and long-distance. These groups had a broad scale of seaborne engagements including trading and raiding. In the NordicBA, world water connected more than it divided. Technologically complex boats were probably superior for long-distance travels, but their production was also more costly in terms of material and labor. Controlling the production of such vessels and outfitting journeys provided another means for chieftains to control long-distance exchange. The returning valuables would then, in turn, increase their status and power as suggested by the hierarchical relationships observed in housing, burials, and metal wealth for Limfjord and Jæren as opposed to Inner Sogn and perhaps Tanum.

8 Conclusion

Enough evidence exists to posit that NordicBA groups encountered other European communities mostly by boat across open water and along coasts, rivers, and lakes. The seaworthiness of all the discussed vessels should not be underestimated as there is ethnographic evidence of unstabilized logboats operating out of sight of the coast (Wright, 2016). Building any boat is a considerable investment in resources, like timbers, resin or tar, material for

---

[1] www.uwarc.de/schiffsfunde/tabellen.php.

ropes, bronze, stone tools, and labor (Sections 5.6 and 6.5). Depending on how production was handled, for example, through collaboration or control, it resulted in different modes of ownership, which was perhaps important for how the potentially considerable returns from expeditions were shared. The estimated carrying capacity of prehistoric vessels demonstrates why the investment was worth it when the expedition was eventually successful. The Bronze Age Ferriby boat, a plank-built vessel discovered in Britain, had a cargo capacity of 5 tons (Wright, 2016). The Hjortspring boat could easily carry 600 kg (Hocker, 2003) so that it can be assumed that its maximum cargo tonnage may be at least 1 ton. The Iron Age logboat found in Hasholme (UK) could have carried cargo of up to 8.6 tons although with a crew reduced to only five members (McGrail, 1988).

While land transport was certainly important, transport capacities, the speed, and the chance to encounter fewer intermediaries or hostile actors may explain why water transport was the most important way that NordicBA communities encountered each other and the rest of Europe. The expected and realized returns probably justified the substantial investments in boatbuilding. However, there is another factor that may have made such expeditions worthwhile. NordicBA communities seem to have frequently encountered their European neighbors in raids and other violent interactions (Horn, 2016; Ling and Cornell, 2010, 2017). The risk of dying or severe injury was considerable through catastrophic failure of boats, hostiles encountered on the way, or even on peaceful expeditions when something went wrong and became violent. With the martial ideology expressed in rock art, sacrifices, and burials especially of high-status individuals, wealth may not have been the only objective of expeditions. The prestige that returning voyages would have brought through the acquisition of highly valued items, but also in reputation for daring a potentially dangerous journey, likely made it worth taking the risk (Helms, 2014). This is yet another parallel that NordicBA communities shared with their Viking Age successors (Kristiansen, 2016a). Apart from supplying the domestic economy with needed resources, successful journeys translated into power and symbolic capital in the political economy.

Our attempt to outline the interlocking systems of the domestic and political economies during the NordicBA (Figure 5) by including local solutions to complex problems has brought the exciting history of this time and region to the fore. It is a story of sea journeys to faraway places in Europe, of a crisis that changed the trajectory of the entire Nordic sphere, and of slavery, warriors, and violence contributing to an ever-shifting and changing sociopolitical landscape. However, it also includes surplus production, for example, through cattle rearing, farming, hunting, and fishing, which allowed local polities to establish their own comparative advantages. Products were exchanged in transregional networks organized by a variety of local power structures ranging from coercive to more communal social formations.

Long-distance trade for copper and tin or exotic goods seems to have been the domain of chiefs and other elites potentially forming alliances to build boats, crew them, and conduct profitable expeditions. To increase the chances of such journeys, instable confederacies may have formed at times along sea routes, mutually assuring the exchange of goods, services, and guest friendship. As we have shown, this system created imbalances among local polities in resources, goods, and labor force which could be redressed through raiding. Raiding also used maritime transport. Here too, alliances were crucial to give raiding parties the highest chance of success. The high mobility for trading and raiding within ever-changing contact networks was probably the biggest contributing factor to the cultural uniformity of the NordicBA sphere that we can observe today.

Many aspects still require further research. Large-scale research combined with rescue excavations of settlements can provide a more complete view of the settled landscape and community organization. Continued work on lead isotopic compositions of metalwork will improve our knowledge about ore sources and potential European trade partners, while studies on aDNA and strontium isotopes may provide evidence of Scandinavians abroad or visitors to Scandinavia. Studies of carbon and nitrogen isotopes as well as lipid analysis of local communities will keep enriching our understanding of local nutrition regiments and how exchange may have supplemented it. While there is little doubt that violent conflict existed during the LBA, our level of understanding of the use of contemporary weaponry is almost missing impeding research on its scale and impact on the economy. We also have a deep understanding of chiefly power through several high-profile excavations of barrows. In micro-regions with stone cairns, the role of burials in the local power structure is less well understood, partly because materials preserve less well there through natural and human destruction. Combined studies of their dating, stone material use, and relationship to settlements would be a large step forward unlocking a deeper understanding of the social formation of local polities. Various case studies and theorizing have shown a need to refine our models to estimate population size and metal influx. Investigations could include abundant depictions of metalwork and estimates of weight of metalwork to gain a better understanding of bronze use where physical finds are lacking. Also important for the discussion is knowledge of Bronze Age boatbuilding from a technological and social standpoint. Studying potential boat remains and construction location should include new surveys, excavations, and ethnographical work to contextualize boat images on rock art panels and metal objects, full-size stone ship settings, and boat-like construction in burial mounds. Ultimately, with these various studies, we could begin to investigate distant partnerships, dependencies, and alliances. The interpretations put forward in synthesis here are just a beginning as we further complicated the story of NordicBA subsistence and political economies.

References

Åberg, N., 1930–1935. Bronzezeitliche und Früheisenzeitliche Chronologie. Kungliga Vitterhets Historie och Antikvitets Akademien, Stockholm.

Allentoft, M. E., Sikora, M., Sjögren, K.-G., et al., 2015. Population genomics of Bronze Age Eurasia. Nature 522 (7555), 167–172.

Amundsen, H. R., 2017. Different Bronze Ages: The emergence of diverging cultural traditions in the southern inland. In Bergerbrant, S., Wessman, A. (eds.), New perspectives on the Bronze Age. Proceedings of the 13th Nordic Bronze Age Symposium held in Gothenburg 9th to 13th June 2015. Archaeopress, Oxford, pp. 343–353.

Andersen, S. H., 1990. Limfjordens forhistorie-en oversigt. Limfjordsprojektet: Rapport: Limjfjordsegnens kulturog naturhistorie 1, 29–65.

Aner, E., Kersten, K., 1973–2017. Funde der älteren Bronzezeit des nordischen Kreises in Dänemark, Schleswig-Holstein und Niedersachsen. Wachholtz, Neumünster.

Anfinset, N., 2015. Metal, Institutions and Economic Structures in Southern Norway during the Early Bronze Age. In Suchowska-Ducke, P., Reiter, S. S., Vandkilde, H. (eds.), Forging identities: The mobility of culture in Bronze Age Europe. BAR International Series 2771–2772. BAR, Oxford, pp. 145–153.

Apel, J., 2001. Daggers, knowledge & power. Uppsala University, Uppsala.

Artursson, M., 2009. Bebyggelse och samhällsstruktur: Södra och mellersta Skandinavien under senneolitikum och bronsålder 2300–500 f. Kr. Gothenburg University, Gothenburg.

Artursson, M., 2015. The long-house as a transforming agent: Emergent complexity in Late Neolithic and Early Bronze Age Southern Scandinavia 2300–1300 BC. In Prieto Martínez, M. P., Salanova, L. (eds.), The Bell Beaker Transition in Europe: Mobility and local evolution during the 3rd millennium BC. Oxbow Books, Havertown, pp. 69–76.

Artursson, M., Björck, N., Larsson, F., 2017. Hus, gård och bygd: bebyggelse, landskap och samhällsorganisation 1100–0 BC. In Artursson, M., Kaliff, A. Larsson, F. (eds.), Rasbobygden i ett långtidsperspektiv, 1100 BC till 1100 AD. kontinuitet och förändring, OPIA 62. Arkeologarna, Uppsala, pp. 35–64.

Artursson, M., Karlenby, L., Larsson, F., 2011. Nibble: En bronsåldersmiljö i Uppland. UV Uppsala Rapport 2011:111. Riksantikvarieämbetet, Uppsala, pp. 1–55.

Austad, I., Hauge, L., Helle, T., Skogen, A., Timberlid, A., 1991. Human-influenced vegetation types and landscape elements in the cultural landscapes of inner Sogn, Western Norway. Norsk Geografisk Tidsskrift: Norwegian Journal of Geography 45 (1), 35–58.

Austvoll, K. I., 2019. Constructing identities: Structure and practice in the Early Bronze Age–Southwest Norway. AmS-Varia 60. University of Stavanger, Stavanger.

Austvoll, K. I., 2020. The emergence of coercive societies in Northwestern Scandinavia during the Late Neolithic–Early Bronze Age. Open Archaeology 6 (1), 19–37.

Austvoll, K. I., 2021. Seaways to complexity: A study of sociopolitical organisation along the coast of Northwestern Scandinavia in the Late Neolithic and Early Bronze Age. New Directions in Anthropological Archaeology. Equinox, Sheffield.

Baudou, E., 1960. Die regionale und chronologische Einteilung der jüngeren Bronzezeit im Nordischen Kreis. Almqvist & Wiksell, Stockholm.

Bakka, E., 1963. Forntida i Odda, Ullensvang og Kinsarvik. In Kolltveit, O. (ed.), Odda, Ullensvang og Kinsarvik i gamal og ny tid. Odda, Ullensvang og Kinsarvik bygdeboknemnd, Bergen, pp. 47–205.

Bakka, E., Kaland, P. E., 1971. Early farming in Hordaland, Western Norway: Problems and approaches in archaeology and pollen analysis. Norwegian Archaeological Review 4 (2), 1–17.

Bech, J.-H., Eriksen, B. V., Kristiansen, K. (eds.), 2018. Bronze age settlement and land-use in Thy, northwest Denmark. Jutland Archaeological Society, 102, Museum Thy, Højbjerg: Jutland Archaeological Society, Thisted, pp. 107–2854.

Becker, C. J., 1964. Neue Hortfunde aus Dänemark mit frühbronzezeitlichen Lanzenspitzen. Acta Archaeologica 35, 115–152.

Bengtsson, B., 2017. Sailing rock art boats: A reassessment of seafaring abilities in Bronze Age Scandinavia and the introduction of the sail in the North. BAR International Series 2865. BAR, Oxford, xvi.

Berger, D., Wang, Q., Brügmann, G., Lockhoff, N., Roberts, B., Pernicka, E., 2022. The Salcombe metal cargoes: New light on the provenance and circulation of tin and copper in Later Bronze Age Europe provided by trace elements and isotopes. Journal of Archeological Science 138, 105543.

Bergerbrant, S., Kristiansen, K., Allentoft, M. E., et al., 2017. Identifying commoners in the Early Bronze Age: Burials outside barrows. In Bergerbrant, S., Wessman, A. (eds.), New perspectives on the Bronze Age. Proceedings of the 13th Nordic Bronze Age Symposium held in Gothenburg 9th to 13th June 2015. Archaeopress, Oxford, pp. 37–64.

Berglund, J., 1982. Kirkebjerget: A Late Bronze Age Settlement at Voldtofte, South-West Funen. Journal of Danish Archaeology 1 (1), 51–63.

Bergström, L., 2004. The Roman Iron Age tar loaf from Albertsro, Sweden: And the Scandinavian tar loaves of the Bronze Age. Acta Archaeologica 75, 1–13.

Binford, L. R., 1962. Archaeology as anthropology. American Antiquity 28 (2), 217–225.

Børsheim, R. L., 2005. Toskipede hus i neolitikum og eldste bronsealder. In Høgestøl, M., Selsing, L., Løken, T., Nærøy, A. J., Prøsch-Danielsen, L. (eds.), Konstruksjonsspor og byggeskikk: Maskinell flateavdekking – metodikk, tolking og forvaltning: [fagseminaret ...]. Varia 43. Arkeologisk Museum, Stavanger, pp. 109–121.

Bradley, R., 2006. Danish razors and Swedish rocks: Cosmology and the Bronze Age landscape. Antiquity 80 (308), 372–389.

Bradley, R., 2022. Maritime archaeology on dry land: Special sites along the coasts of Britain and Ireland from the first farmers to the Atlantic Bronze Age, Paperback ed. Oxbow Books, Philadelphia.

Brink, K., 2013. Houses and hierarchies: Economic and social relations in the Late Neolithic and Early Bronze Age of Southernmost Scandinavia. European Journal of Archaeology 16 (3), 433–458.

Brink, K., 2015. Farms and villages in the Late Neolithic and earliest Bronze Age of Southernmost Scandinavia: Examples from Southwest Scania, Sweden. In Suchowska-Ducke, P., Reiter, S. S., Vandkilde, H. (eds.), Forging identities: The mobility of culture in Bronze Age Europe. BAR International Series 2771–2772. BAR, Oxford, pp. 167–174.

Brinker, U., Flohr, S., Hauenstein, K., et al., 2014. Die menschlichen Skelettreste aus dem Tollensetal: Ein Vorbericht. In Jantzen, D., Orschiedt, J., Piek, J., Terberger, T. (eds.), Tod im Tollensetal. Forschungen zu den Hinterlassenschaften eines bronzezeitlichen Gewaltkonfliktes in Mecklenburg-Vorpommern. Beiträge zur Ur- und Frühgeschichte Mecklenburg- Vorpommerns 50. Landesamt für Kultur und Denkmalpflege Mecklenburg-Vorpommern, Schwerin, pp. 191–208.

Brinker, U., Schramm, A., Jantzen, D., et al., 2016. The Bronze Age battlefield in the Tollense Valley, Mecklenburg-Western Pomerania, Northeast Germany: Combat marks on human bones as evidence of early warrior societies in northern Middle Europe? In Coimbra, F., Delfino, D., Sîrbu, V., Schuster, C. (eds.), Late prehistory and protohistory: Bronze Age and Iron Age. Proceedings of the XVII UISPP World Congress (1–7 September 2014, Burgos, Spain). Archaeopress, Oxford, pp. 39–56.

Brøgger, A. W., 1925. Det norske folk i oldtiden. Instituttet for sammenlignende kulturforskning, Oslo.

Broholm, H. C., 1944. Kultur og folk i den ældre bronzealder: Danmarks Bronzealder. Nyt nordisk forlag, Copenhagen.

Brumfiel, E. M., 1987. Elite and utilitarian crafts in the Aztec state. In Brumfiel, E. M., Earle, T. K. (eds.), Specialization, exchange and complex societies. New directions in archaeology. Cambridge University Press, Cambridge, pp. 102–118.

Brumfiel, E. M., Earle, T. K. (eds.), 1987. Specialization, exchange and complex societies: New directions in archaeology. Cambridge University Press, Cambridge.

Bunnefeld, J.-H., 2016. Älterbronzezeitliche Vollgriffschwerter in Dänemark und Schleswig-Holstein. Wachholtz, Neumünster.

Bunnefeld, J.-H., 2018. The chief and his sword? Some thoughts on the swordbearer's rank in the Early Nordic Bronze Age. In Horn, C., Kristiansen, K. (eds.), Warfare in Bronze Age society. Cambridge University Press, Cambridge, pp. 198–212.

Callanan, M. E., 2014. Bronze age arrows from Norwegian alpine snow patches. Journal of Glacial Archaeology 1 (1), 25–49.

Catling, C., 2010. Raiders and traders: New research on the Vikings. Current archaeology (245), 12–21.

Champion, T. C. E., 1989. Introduction. In Champion, T. C. E. (ed.), Centre and periphery: Comparative studies in archaeology. Unwin Hyman, London, pp. 1–20.

Chernela, J., 2008. Guesting, feasting and raiding: Transformations of violence in the Northwest Amazon. In Beckerman, S., Valentine, P. (eds.), Revenge in the cultures of lowland South America. University Press of Florida, Gainesville, pp. 42–59.

Childe, V. G., 1925. The dawn of European civilization. Keegan Paul, London.

Childe, V. G., 1931. The Bronze Age. Cambridge University Press, Cambridge.

Childe, V. G., 1951. Social Evolution. Watts, London.

Clarke, D. L., 1971. Analytical archaeology. Methuen, London.

Clark, P. (ed.), 2004. The Dover Bronze Age boat in context: Society and water transport in prehistoric Europe. Oxbow, Oxford.

Crumlin-Pedersen, O., Trakadas, A. (eds.), 2003. Hjortspring: A Pre-Roman Iron-Age warship in context. Viking Ship Museum, Roskilde.

Cunliffe, B. W., Durham, E., Cartwright, I. R., 2019. Sark: A sacred island? Oxford University School of Archaeology monograph 81. School of Archaeology, Oxford.

Dahl, B. I., 2014. Arkeologisk utgraving av hus og graver: Myklebust gnr. 3, Sola kommune, Rogaland. Museum of Archaeology Stavanger, Stavanger.

Dahlström, Å., Brost, L., 1996. The amber book. Geoscience Press, Tuscan.

Dalsgaard, K., Nielsen, M. W., 2018. Were the Bronze Age fields at Bjerre 4 manured? A survey of the phosphorus content and a comment on the cultivation potential. In Bech, J.-H., Eriksen, B. V., Kristiansen, K. (eds.), Bronze age settlement and land-use in Thy, Northwest Denmark. Museum Thy, Højbjerg, pp. 459–468.

D'Altroy, T. N., Earle, T. K., 1985. Staple finance, wealth finance, and storage in the Inka political economy. Current Anthropology 26 (2), 187–206.

Davies, G., 2016. A history of money: From ancient times to the present day, Fourth edition (revised ed.) University of Wales Press, Cardiff.

Demange, M., 2012. Mineralogy for petrologists: Optics, chemistry, and occurrences of rock-forming minerals. CRC Press, Boca Raton.

DeMarrais, E., Earle, T., 2017. Collective action theory and the dynamics of complex societies. Annual Review of Anthropology 46 (1), 183–201.

Denham, S., Høgestøl, M., Lillehammer, G., 2018. A search through the archives: Looking for the young and the old in a museum's collections. In Lillehammer, G., Murphy, E.M. (eds.), Across the generations: The old and the young in past societies. Proceedings from the 22nd Annual Meeting of the EAA in Vilnius, Lithuania, 31st August–4th September 2016. Arkeologisk museum i Stavanger, Stavanger, pp. 77–90.

Díaz-Guardamino, M., Ling, J., Koch, J., et al., 2022. The local appropriation of warrior ideals in Late Bronze Age Europe: A review of the rock art site of Arroyo Tamujoso 8 and the "warrior" stela of Cancho Roano (Badajoz, Spain). Trabajos de Prehistoria 79 (2), 329–345. https://doi.org/10.3989/tp.2022.12302.

Diinhoff, S., 2005. Den vestnorske agrarbosætning: Fra sen stenalder til folkevandringstid: Arkeologiske resultater fra et tiår med fladeafdækninger på Vestlandet. In Høgestøl, M., Selsing, L., Løken, T., Nærøy, A. J., Prøsch-Danielsen, L. (eds.), Konstruksjonsspor og byggeskikk: Maskinell flateavdekking – metodikk, tolking og forvaltning. Arkeologisk Museum, Stavanger, pp. 75–85.

Diinhoff, S., 2013. Jordbruksbosætning på Vestlandet: Nogle statistiske betragtninger. In Diinhoff, S., Ramstad, M., Slinning, T. (eds.), Jordbruksbosetningens utvikling på Vestlandet. Seminar om dagens kunnskapsstatus, presentasjon av nye resultater og fremtidige problemstillinger. Universitetet i Bergen, Bergen, pp. 53–64.

Earle, T., 1978. Economic and social organization of a complex chiefdom. University of Michigan Press, Ann Arbor.

Earle, T., 2010. Exchange systems in prehistory. In Dillian, C.D., White, C.L. (eds.), Trade and exchange. Archaeological studies from history and prehistory. Springer, New York, pp. 205–217.

Earle, T., 2017. Chiefs, chieftaincies, chiefdoms, and chiefly confederacies: Power in the evolution of political systems. In Carneiro, R. L., Grinin, L. E., Korotaev, A. V. (eds.), Chiefdoms. Yesterday and today. Eliot Werner, New York, pp. 233–256.

Earle, T., 2021. A primer on chiefs and chiefdoms. Principles of archaeology. Eliot Werner, Clinton Corners.

Earle, T., Bech, J.-H., Kristiansen, K., Aperlo, P., Kelertas, K., Steinberg, J., 1998. The Political Economy of Late Neolithic and Early Bronze Age Society: The Thy Archaeological Project. Norwegian Archaeological Review 31 (1), 1-28.

Earle, T., Ling, J., Uhnér, C., Stos-Gale, Z., Melheim, L., 2015. The political economy and metal trade in Bronze Age Europe: Understanding regional variability in terms of comparative advantages and articulations. European Journal of Archaeology 18 (4), 633–657.

Earle, T., Olsen, A.-L. H., Eriksen, B. V., Henriksen, P. S., Kristensen, I. K., 2022. Everyday Life at Bjerre Site 7, a Late Bronze Age House in Thy, Denmark. European Journal of Archaeology 25 (3), 372–395.

Earle, T., Bech, J.-H., Villa, C., 2023. New Early Neolithic and Late Bronze Age amber finds from Thy. Antiquity 97 (391), 70-85.

Earle, T. K., 2002. Bronze Age economics: The beginnings of political economies. Westview, Boulder.

Earle, T. K., 2019. An essay on political economies in prehistory. Eliot Werner, Clinton Corners.

Effenberger, H., 2018. The plant economy of the Northern European Bronze Age: More diversity through increased trade with southern regions. Vegetation History and Archaeobotany 27 (1), 65–74.

Eichfeld, I., 2020. Aus Aller und Ise: Alte Einbäume neu datiert. Archäologie in Niedersachsen 23, 57–61.

Engels, F., 1942. The origin of the family, private property, and the state, in the light of the researches of Lewis H. Morgan. International, New York, pp. 285.

Eriksen, M. H., Austvoll, K. I., 2020. Bridging perspectives: Social dynamics of houses and households in the Nordic Bronze Age. In Austvoll, K. I., Melheim, A. L., Eriksen, M. H., et al. (eds.), Contrasts of the Bronze Age: Time, trajectories and encounters in the Nordic World. Essays in Honour of Christopher Prescott. Brepols, Turnhout, pp. 187–201.

Ethelberg, P., 2000. Bronzealderen. In Ethelberg, P., Jørgensen, E., Meier, D., Robinson, D. (eds.), Det Sønderjyske landbrugs historie. Sten- og bronzealder. Haderslev Museum og Historisk Samfund for Sønderjylland, Haderslev, pp. 135–280.

Fauvelle, M., 2013. Evaluating cross-channel exchange in the Santa Barbara region: Experimental data on acorn processing and transport. American Antiquity 78 (4), 790–798.

Feinman, G. M., 2017. Multiple pathways to large-scale human cooperative networks: A reframing. In Chacon, R. J., Mendoza, R. G. (eds.), Feast, famine or fighting? Studies in human ecology and adaptation. Springer International, Cham, pp. 459–478.

Feinman, G. M., Neitzel, J., 1984. Too many types: An overview of Sedentary Prestate Societies in the Americas. Advances in Archaeological Method and Theory 7, 39–102.

Felding, L., 2016. The Egtved girl: Trade travel and alliance in the Bronze Age. Adoranten 2015, 5–20.

Floderus, E., 1931. Ett gotländskt ekkistfynd från bronsåldern. Fornvännen 26, 284–290.

Frei, K. M., Villa, C., Jørkov, M. L., et al., 2017. A matter of months: High precision migration chronology of a Bronze Age female. PloS One 12 (6), e0178834.

Fyllingen, H., 2003. Society and violence in the Early Bronze Age: An analysis of human skeletons from Nord-Trøndelag, Norway. Norwegian Archaeological Review 36 (1), 27–43.

Fyllingen, H., 2006. Society and the structure of violence: A story told by Middle Bronze Age human remains from central Norway. In Otto, T., Thrane, H., Vandkilde, H. (eds.), Warfare and society. Archaeological and social anthropological perspectives. Aarhus University Press, Aarhus, pp. 319–329.

Fyllingen, H., 2012. Arkeologisk utgravning på Tjora, gnr. 10 bnr. 5,17, og 19: Sola kommune, Rogaland: Sesong 2008–2009. Museum of Archaeology Stavanger, Stavanger.

Fyllingen, H., 2015. Jåsundundersøkelsene i 2010–2011: Et innblikk i samfunnsutviklingen nord på Tanangerhalvøya, Sola kommune 7000 f.Kr.–500 e.Kr. Museum of Archaeology Stavanger, Stavanger.

Gamble, L. H., 2008. The Chumash world at European contact: Power, trade, and feasting among complex hunter-gatherers. University of California Press, Berkeley.

Garfinkel, M. R., Skaperdas, S., 2007. Economics of conflict: An overview. In Sandler, T., Hartley, K. (eds.), Handbook of Defense Economics .Defense in a Globalized World, vol. 2. Handbook of Defense Economics 2. Elsevier, Amsterdam, pp. 649–709.

Gebauer, A. B., Sørensen, L. V., Taube, M., Wielandt, D. K. P., 2021. First metallurgy in Northern Europe: An early Neolithic crucible and a possible Tuyère from Lønt, Denmark. European Journal of Archaeology 24 (1), 27–47.

Gilman, A., 1981. The development of social stratification in Bronze Age Europe. Current Anthropology 22 (1), 1–23.

Gilman, A., 1995. Prehistoric European chiefdoms. In Price, T. D., Feinman, G. M. (eds.), Foundations of social inequality. Fundamental issues in archaeology. Springer, New York, pp. 235–251.

Gjerde, J. M., 2010. Rock art and landscapes: Studies of Stone Age rock art from northern Fennoscandia. PhD. University of Tromsø, Tromsø.

Gjessing, G., 1945. Norges steinalder. Norsk arkeologisk selskap, Oslo.

Godelier, M., 1999. The enigma of the gift. University of Chicago Press, Chicago.

Goldhahn, J., 1999. Rock art and the materialization of a cosmology: The case of the Sagaholm barrow. In Goldhahn, J. (ed.), Rock art as social representation. Archaeopress, Oxford, pp. 77–100.

Goldhahn, J., 2006. Från landskapets monument till monumentens landskap: Om döda och efterlevande med exempel från äldre bronsålder, 1700–1100 BC. In Østigård, T. (ed.), Lik og ulik. Tilnærminger til variasjon i gravskikk. University of Bergen, Bergen, pp. 171–202.

Goldhahn, J., Ling, J., 2013. Bronze Age rock art in Northern Europe: Contexts and interpretations. In Fokkens, H., Harding, A. F. (eds.), The Oxford handbook of the European Bronze Age. Oxford University Press, Oxford, pp. 270–290.

Goldhahn, J., Østigård, T. (eds.), 2007. Rituelle spesialister i bronse- og jernalderen. GOTARC Serie C, Arkeologiska skrifter. Inst. för arkeologi och antikens kultur Göteborgs universitet, Göteborg, p. 1-382.

Goldhammer, J., 2015. Studien zu Steinartefakten der Bronzezeit: Siedlungsinventare aus Nord- und Südschleswig im Vergleich. Wachholtz, Neumünster.

Gouldner, A. W., 1960. The norm of reciprocity: A preliminary statement. American Sociological Review 25 (2), 161–178.

Gron, K. J., Larsson, M., Gröcke, D. R., et al., 2021. Archaeological cereals as an isotope record of long-term soil health and anthropogenic amendment in southern Scandinavia. Quaternary Science Reviews 253, 106762.

Gron, K. J., Montgomery, J., Rowley-Conwy, P., 2015. Cattle management for dairying in Scandinavia's Earliest Neolithic. PloS One 10 (7), e0131267.

Haak, W., Lazaridis, I., Patterson, N., et al., 2015. Massive migration from the steppe was a source for Indo-European languages in Europe. Nature 522 (7555), 207–211.

Haavelmo, T., 1956. Study in the theory of economic evolution. North-Holland, Amsterdam.

Hagen, A., 1983. Norges oldtid. Cappelens, Oslo.

Halvorsen, L. S., 2005. Prosjekt E 39 Hjelle, Eid kommune, Sogn og Fjordane: Palaeobotanical report. University Museum of Bergen, Bergen.

Halvorsen, L. S., 2006. Prosjekt Torvund – Teigen: Paleobotanisk undersøkelse ved Torvund og Norevik, Høyanger, Sogn og Fjordane: Palaeobotanical report. University Museum of Bergen, Bergen.

Halvorsen, L. S., 2008. Makrofossilanalyse fra Sæla gbn. 94/2 og 4, Naustdal, Sogn og Fjordane: Palaeobotanical report. University Museum of Bergen, Bergen.

Hansen, S., 2022. Long-distance interaction in fourth millennium BCE Eurasia. In Ling, J., Chacon, R. J., Kristiansen, K. (eds.), Trade before civilization. Long Distance Exchange and the Rise of Social Complexity. Cambridge University Press, Cambridge, pp. 334–360.

Harding, A., 2021. Salt: White gold in early Europe. Cambridge University Press, Cambridge.

Harding, A., Hughes-Brock, H., Beck, C. W., 1974. Amber in the Mycenaean world. The Annual of the British School at Athens 69, 145–172.

Harding, A. F., 2017. Salt in prehistoric Europe. Sidestone Press, Leiden.

Helms, M. W., 2014. Ancient Panama. Chiefs in search of power. University of Texas Press, Austin.

Helskog, K., 1999. The shore connection: Cognitive landscape and communication with rock carvings in Northernmost Europe. Norwegian Archaeological Review 32 (2), 73–94.

Hendrickson, D., Armon, J., Mearns, R., 1998. The changing nature of conflict and famine vulnerability: The case of livestock raiding in Turkana District, Kenya. Disasters 22 (3), 185–199.

Henriksen, P. S., Robinson, D. E., Kelertas, K., 2018. Bronze Age agriculture, land use and vegetation at Bjerre Enge based on the results of archaeobotanical analyses. In Bech, J.-H., Eriksen, B. V., Kristiansen, K. (eds.), Bronze age settlement and land-use in Thy, northwest Denmark. Museum Thy & Jutland Archaeological Society, Højbjerg & Thisted, pp. 387–458.

Hirshleifer, J., 1995. Anarchy and its breakdown. Journal of Political Economy 103 (1), 26–52.

Hjelle, K.L., 2003. Botanisk rapport: Rutlin gbnr 22/4, Sogndal kommune, Sogn og Fjordane: Palaeobotanical report. University Museum of Bergen, Bergen.

Hjelle, K. L., 2005. Pollenanalyse av prøver på "Kvålslid Aust," Sogndal kommune, Sogn og Fjordane: Palaeobotanical report. University Museum of Bergen, Bergen.

Hjelle, K. L., Hufthammer, A. K., Bergsvik, K. A., 2006. Hesitant hunters: A review of the introduction of agriculture in Western Norway. Environmental Archaeology 11 (2), 147–170.

Hocker, F. M., 2003. Documentation and calculation of boat characteristics. In Crumlin-Pedersen, O., Trakadas, A. (eds.), Hjortspring. A Pre-Roman Iron-Age warship in context. Viking Ship Museum, Roskilde, pp. 84–118.

Høgestøl, M., 2003. Ei gåtefull massegrav . . . Viking 66, 105–108.

Høgestøl, M., Prøsch-Danielsen, L., 2006. Impulses of agro-pastoralism in the 4th and 3rd millennia BC on the south-western coastal rim of Norway. Environmental Archaeology 11 (1), 19–34.

Holck, P., 1987. Kråkerøy: Et gammelt kriminalmysterium? Borgarsyssel Museums Årbok, 31–42.

Holst, M. K., Breuning-Madsen, H., Rasmussen, M., 2001. The South Scandinavian barrows with well- preserved oak-log coffins. Antiquity 75 (287), 126–136.

Holst, M. K., Rasmussen, M., 2013. Herder communities: Longhouses, cattle and landscape organization in the Nordic Early and Middle Bronze Age. In Sabatini, S., Bergerbrant, S. (eds.), Counterpoint. Essays in archaeology and heritage studies in honour of Professor Kristian Kristiansen. Archaeopress, Oxford, pp. 99–110.

Holst, M. K., Rasmussen, M., Kristiansen, K., Bech, J.-H., 2013. Bronze Age "Herostrats": Ritual, political, and domestic economies in Early Bronze Age Denmark. Proceedings of the Prehistoric Society 79, 265–296.

Horn, C., 2013. Weapons, fighters and combat: Spears and swords in Early Bronze Age Scandinavia. Danish Journal of Archaeology 2 (1), 20–44.

Horn, C., 2014. Studien zu den europäischen Stabdolchen. Universitätsforschungen zur Prähistorischen Archäologie 246. Habelt, Bonn.

Horn, C., 2015. Combat and Change: Remarks on Early Bronze Age spears from Sweden. In Suchowska- Ducke, P., Reiter, S. S., Vandkilde, H. (eds.), Forging identities: The mobility of culture in Bronze Age Europe, vol. 2. BAR, Oxford, pp. 201–212.

Horn, C., 2016. Nothing to lose: Waterborne raiding in southern Scandinavia. In Glørstad, H., Tsigaridas Glørstad, A. Z., Melheim, L. (eds.), Comparative perspectives on past colonisation, maritime interaction and cultural integration. Equinox, Sheffield, pp. 109–127.

Horn, C., 2018a. Die by the sword … or the spear? Early bronze weapons in Scandinavia. In Fernández- Götz, M., Roymans, N. (eds.), Conflict archaeology. Materials of collective violence from prehistory to late antiquity. Routledge, London, pp. 51–60.

Horn, C., 2018b. Warfare vs. Exchange? Thoughts on an Integrative Approach. In Horn, C., Kristiansen, K. (eds.), Warfare in Bronze Age society. Cambridge University Press, Cambridge, pp. 47–60.

Horn, C., 2023. Warriors as a challenge: Violence, rock art, and the preservation of social cohesion during the Nordic Bronze Age. European Journal of Archaeology 26 (1), 57–80.

Horn, C., Karck, T., 2019. Weapon and tool use during the Nordic Bronze Age. Danish Journal of Archaeology 8, 1–20.

Horn, C., Kristiansen, K., 2018. Introducing Bronze Age warfare. In Horn, C., Kristiansen, K. (eds.), Warfare in Bronze Age society. Cambridge University Press, Cambridge, pp. 1–15.

Hornell, J., 2014. Water transport: Origins and early evolution. Cambridge University Press, Cambridge.

Hornstrup, K. M., 2017. From bird wings to fool's gold: Organic materials and stone from burials of the Late Bronze Age. In Bergerbrant, S., Wessman, A. (eds.), New perspectives on the Bronze Age. Proceedings of the 13th Nordic Bronze Age Symposium held in Gothenburg 9th to 13th June 2015. Archaeopress, Oxford, pp. 81–93.

Hufthammer, A. K., 2015. Osteological assemblages from rock shelters as source data for subsistence from Bronze Age to the Middle Ages in Western Norway. In Indrelid, S., Hjelle, K.L., Stene, K. (eds.), Exploitation of outfield resources. University of Bergen & University Museum of Bergen, Bergen, pp. 231–240.

Isaksson, S., 2009. Vessels of change: A long-term perspective on prehistoric pottery use in southern and eastern middle Sweden based on lipid residue analyses. Current Swedish Archaeology 17, 131–149.

Iversen, R., 2017. Big-men and small chiefs: The creation of Bronze Age societies. Open Archaeology 3 (1), 234–375.

Jantzen, D., Brinker, U., Orschiedt, J., et al., 2011. A Bronze Age battlefield? Weapons and trauma in the Tollense Valley, north-eastern Germany. Antiquity 85 (328), 417–433.

Jantzen, D., Orschiedt, J., Piek, J., Terberger, T. (eds.), 2014. Tod im Tollensetal: Forschungen zu den Hinterlassenschaften eines bronzezeitlichen

Gewaltkonfliktes in Mecklenburg-Vorpommern. Landesamt für Kultur und Denkmalpflege Mecklenburg-Vorpommern, Schwerin, 274 S.

Jensen, J., 2001. Danmarks Oldtid: Stenalder, 13000–2000 f. Kr. Gyldendal, Copenhagen.

Johansen, Ø. K., 1993. Norske depotfunn fra bronsealderen. University of Oslo, Oslo.

Kastholm, O. T., 2015. Plankboat skeuomorphs in Bronze Age logboats: A Scandinavian perspective. Antiquity 89 (348), 1353–1372.

Kaul, F., 1998. Ships on bronzes: A study in Bronze Age religion and iconography Studies in archaeology & history, vol. 3. National Museum of Denmark, Copenhagen.

Kaul, F., 2003. The Hjortspring boat and ship iconography of the Bronze Age and Early Pre-Roman Iron Age. In Crumlin-Pedersen, O., Trakadas, A. (eds.), Hjortspring. A Pre-Roman Iron-Age warship in context. Viking Ship Museum, Roskilde, pp. 187–207.

Kaul, F., 2017. The xenia concept of guest-friendship: Providing an elucidatory model for Bronze Age communication. In Skoglund, P., Ling, J., Bertilsson, U. (eds.), North meets south: Theoretical aspects on the northern and southern rock art. Swedish rock art Series 6. Oxbow Books, Oxford, pp. 172–198.

Kjær, H., 1912. Et mærkeligt arkæologisk-antropologisk Fund fra Stenalderen. Aarbøger for Nordisk Oldkyndighed og Historie 2, 58–72.

Kradin, N. N., 2015. Nomadic empires in Inner Asia. In Bemmann, J., Schmauder, M. (eds.), Complexity of interaction along the Eurasian Steppe zone in the first Millennium CE. Rheinische Friedrich-Wilhelms- Universität Bonn, Bonn, pp. 11–48.

Kristiansen, K., 1984. Krieger und Häuptlinge in der Bronzezeit Dänemarks: Ein Beitrag zur Geschichte des bronzezeitlichen Schwertes. Jahrbuch des Römisch-Germanischen Zentralmuseums Mainz 31, 187–208.

Kristiansen, K., 1987. Centre and periphery in Bronze Age Scandinavia. In Rowlands, M. J., Larsen, M., Kristiansen, K. (eds.), Centre and periphery in the ancient world. New directions in archaeology. Cambridge University Press, Cambridge, pp. 74–86.

Kristiansen, K., 1989. Value, ranking and consumption in the Bronze Age. In Nordström, H.-Å., Knape, A. (eds.), Bronze Age studies. Statens Historiska Museum, Stockholm, pp. 21–24.

Kristiansen, K., 2000. Europe before history: New studies in archaeology. Cambridge University Press, Cambridge.

Kristiansen, K., 2002. The tale of the sword: Swords and swordfighters in Bronze Age Europe. Oxford Journal of Archeology 21 (4), 319–332.

Kristiansen, K., 2006. Cosmology, economy and long-term change in the Bronze Age of Northern Europe. In Sjögren, K.-G. (ed.), Ecology and economy in Stone and Bronze Age Scania. Skånska spår–arkeologi längs Västkustbanen. Riksantikvarieämbetet, Stockholm, pp. 170–218.

Kristiansen, K., 2007. The rules of the game: Decentralised complexity and power structures. In Kohring, S., Wynne-Jones, S. (eds.), Socialising complexity. Approaches to power and interaction in the archaeological record. Oxbow Books, Oxford, 60–75.

Kristiansen, K., 2010. Decentralized complexity: The case of Bronze Age Northern Europe. In Price, T. D., Feinman, G. M. (eds.), Pathways to power: New perspectives on the emergence of social inequality. Springer, New York, pp. 169–192.

Kristiansen, K., 2014. Towards a new paradigm: The third science revolution and its possible consequences in archaeology. Current Swedish Archaeology 22, 11-71.

Kristiansen, K., 2016a. Bronze Age Vikings? A comparative analysis of deep historical structures and their dynamics. In Glørstad, H., Glørstad, A. Z. T., Melheim, L. (eds.), Comparative perspectives on past colonisation, maritime interaction and cultural integration. Equinox, Sheffield, pp. 177–186.

Kristiansen, K., 2016b. Interpreting Bronze Age trade and migration. In Kiriatzi, E., Knappett, C. (eds.), Human mobility and technological transfer in the prehistoric Mediterranean. British School at Athens studies in Greek antiquity. Cambridge University Press, Cambridge, pp. 154–181.

Kristiansen, K., 2018. Warfare and the political economy: Europe 1500–1100 BC. In Horn, C., Kristiansen, K. (eds.), Warfare in Bronze Age society. Cambridge University Press, Cambridge, pp. 23–46.

Kristiansen, K., 2022. Bronze Age globalisation in numbers: Volumes of trade and its organisation. In Hofmann, D., Nikulka, F., Schuhmann, R. (eds.), Baltic in the Bronze Age. Regional patterns, interactions and boundaries. Sidestone, Leiden, pp. 1–20.

Kristiansen, K., Larsson, T. B., 2005. The rise of Bronze Age society: Travels, transmissions and transformations. Cambridge University Press, Cambridge.

Kristiansen, K., Melheim, L., Bech, J.-H., Mortensen, M. F., Frei, K. M., 2020. Thy at the crossroads: A local Bronze Age community's role in a macro-economic system. In Austvoll, K. I., Melheim, A. L., Eriksen, M. H., et al. (eds.), Contrasts of the Bronze Age: Time, trajectories and encounters in the Nordic World. Essays in honour of Christopher Prescott. Brepols, Turnhout, pp. 269–282.

Kristiansen, K., Suchowska-Ducke, P., 2015. Connected histories: The dynamics of Bronze Age interaction and trade 1500–1100 BC. Proceedings of the Prehistoric Society 81, 361–392.

Lankton, J. W., Pulak, C., Gratuze, B., 2022. Glass ingots from the Uluburun shipwreck: Glass by the batch in the Late Bronze Age. Journal of Archaeological Science: Reports 42, 103354.

Larsen, C. I., 1997. Haugene fra eldre bronsealder på Jæren: En religionsarkeologisk analyse. In Fuglestvedt, I., Myhre, B. (eds.), Konflikt i forhistorien. Arkeologisk museum i Stavanger, Stavanger, pp. 15–26.

Larsson, T. B., 1986. The Bronze Age metalwork in southern Sweden: Aspects of social and spatial organization 1800–500 B.C. Archaeology and environment 6. University of Umeå, Umeå.

Larsson, T. B., 1989. Bronze!: Power and wealth in Early Bronze Age Scania. In Nordström, H.-Å., Knape, A. (eds.), Bronze Age studies. Statens Historiska Museum, Stockholm, pp. 25–44.

Lemonnier, P., 1991. From great men to big men: Peace, substitution and competition in the Highlands of New Guinea. In Godelier, M., Strathern, M. (eds.), Big men and great men. Personifications of power in Melanesia. Cambridge University Press, Cambridge etc., pp. 7–27.

Lindström, J., 2009. Bronsåldersmordet: Om arkeologi och ond bråd död. Norstedt, Stockholm.

Ling, J., 2012. War canoes or social units? Human representation in rock-art ships. European Journal of Archaeology 15 (3), 465–485.

Ling, J., 2014. Elevated rock art: Towards a maritime understanding of Bronze Age rock art in northern Bohuslan, Sweden. Oxbow Books, Oxford.

Ling, J., Chacon, R. J., Chacon, Y., 2018a. Rock art, secret societies, long-distance exchange, and warfare in Bronze Age Scandinavia. In Dolfini, A., Crellin, R. J., Horn, C., Uckelmann, M. (eds.), Prehistoric warfare and violence. Quantitative and Qualitative Approaches. Springer, Cham, pp. 149–174.

Ling, J., Earle, T., Kristiansen, K., 2018b. Maritime mode of production: Raiding and trading in seafaring chiefdoms. Current Anthropology 59 (5), 488–524.

Ling, J., Chacon, R. J., Chacon, Y., 2021. Rock art and nautical routes to social complexity: Comparing Haida and Scandinavian Bronze Age societies. Adoranten 2020, 5-23.

Ling, J., Chacon, R. J., Kristiansen, K. (eds.), 2022. Trade before civilization: Long distance exchange and the rise of social complexity. Cambridge University Press, Cambridge.

Ling, J., Cornell, P., 2010. Rock art as secondary agent? Society and agency in Bronze Age Bohuslän. Norwegian Archaeological Review 43 (1), 26–43.

Ling, J., Cornell, P., 2017. Violence, warriors, and rock art in Bronze Age Scandinavia. In Chacon, R. J., Mendoza, R. G. (eds.), Feast, famine or fighting?, vol. 8. Studies in Human Ecology and Adaptation. Springer International, Cham, pp. 15–33.

Ling, J., Cornell, P., Kristiansen, K., 2017. Bronze economy and mode of production: The role of comparative advantages in temperate Europe during. In Rosenswig, R. M., Cunningham, J. J. (eds.), Modes of production and archaeology. University Press of Florida, Gainesville, pp. 205–230.

Ling, J., Hjärthner-Holdar, E., Grandin, L., et al., 2019. Moving metals IV: Swords, metal sources and trade networks in Bronze Age Europe. Journal of Archaeological Science: Reports 26, 101837.

Ling, J., Rowlands, M., 2013. Boundaries, flows and connectivities: Mobility and stasis in the Bronze Age. In Sabatini, S., Bergerbrant, S. (eds.), Counterpoint. Essays in archaeology and heritage studies in honour of Professor Kristian Kristiansen. Archaeopress, Oxford, pp. 517–530.

Ling, J., Stos-Gale, Z., Grandin, L., et al., 2014. Moving metals II: Provenancing Scandinavian Bronze Age artefacts by lead isotope and elemental analyses. Journal of Archaeological Science 41, 106–132.

Ling, J., Uhnér, C., 2014. Rock art and metal trade. Adoranten 21, 23–43.

Løken, T., 1987. En bronsealderboplass med kokesteinsrøys, og huskonstruksjon på Løbrekk i Strand. Frá haug ok heiðni 2, 190–194.

Løken, T., 2021. Bronze Age and Early Iron Age house and settlement development at Forsandmoen, south-western Norway. Archaeological Museum Stavanger, Stavanger.

Lund, J., Furholt, M., Austvoll, K. I., 2022. Re-assessing power in the archaeological discourse: How collective, cooperative and affective perspectives may impact our understanding of social relations and organization in prehistory. Archaeological Dialogues 29 (1), 33-50.

Mandt, G., 1991. Vestnorske ristninger i tid og rom: Kronologiske, korologiske og kontekstuelle studier. PhD. Unniversity of Bergen, Bergen.

Marstrander, S., 1963. Østfolds jordbruksristninger: Skjeberg. Universitetsforlaget Oslo.

Marx, K., 1953. Grundrisse der Kritik der politischen Ökonomie (Rohentwurf). Dietz, Berlin.

Mauss, M., 2010. Soziologie und Anthropologie. VS Verl. für Sozialwissenschaften, Wiesbaden.

McGrail, S., 1988. Assessing the performance of an ancient boat? The Hasholme logboat. Oxford Journal of Archaeology 7 (1), 35–46.

McKinley, J. I., Leivers, M., Schuster, J., et al., 2014. Cliffs end farm, Isle of Thanet, Kent: A mortuary and ritual site of the Bronze Age, Iron Age and Anglo-Saxon period with evidence for long-distance maritime mobility. Wessex Archaeology, Salisbury.

Melheim, A. L., Ling, J., 2017. Taking the stranger on board: The two maritime legacies of Bronze Age rock art. In Skoglund, P., Ling, J., Bertilsson, U. (eds.), North meets south. Theoretical aspects on the northern and southern rock art. Oxbow Books, Oxford, pp. 59–86.

Melheim, L., Grandin, L., Persson, P.-O., et al., 2018. Moving metals III: Possible origins for copper in Bronze Age Denmark based on lead isotopes and geochemistry. Journal of Archaeological Science 96, 85–105.

Melheim, L., Prescott, C., Anfinset, N., 2016. Bronze casting and cultural connections: Bronze Age workshops at Hunn, Norway. Praehistorische Zeitschrift 91 (1), 42–67.

Mikkelsen, M., 2020. Slaves in Bronze Age southern Scandinavia? Acta Archaeologica 91 (1), 147–190.

Mikkelsen, M., Kristiansen, K., 2018. Legaard. In Bech, J.-H., Eriksen, B. V., Kristiansen, K. (eds.), Bronze Age settlement and land-use in Thy, northwest Denmark. Museum Thy & Jutland Archaeological Society, Højbjerg & Thisted, pp. 505–538.

Moen, A., Lillethun, A., Odland, A., 1999. National atlas of Norway: Vegetation. Norwegian Mapping Authority, Hønefoss.

Møllerop, O. J., 1962. Fra Rogalands eldre bronsealder. Stavanger Museums Årbok, pp. 5–58.

Molloy, B., Horn, C., 2020. Weapons, warriors and warfare in Bronze Age Europe. In Fagan, G. G., Fibiger, L., Hudson, M., Trundle, M. (eds.), The Cambridge World History of violence. The Prehistoric and Ancient worlds. Cambridge University Press, Cambridge, pp. 117–141.

Montelius, O., 1881. Om den nordiska bronsålderns ornamentik och dess betydelse för frågan om periodens indelning. Vitterhets Hist. och Antiqvitets Akademiens Månadsblad 1881, 17–71.

Montelius, O., 1885. Om tidsbestämning inom bronsåldern med särskilt avseende på Skandinavien. Kungl. Vitterhets Historie och Antikvitets Akademien. Stockholm.

Mukherjee, A. J., Roßberger, E., James, M. A., et al., 2008. The Qatna lion: Scientific confirmation of Baltic amber in Late Bronze Age Syria. Antiquity 82 (315), 49–59.

Müller, S., 1877. Bronzealderens perioder: En Undersøgelse i forhistorisk Archæologi. Aarbøger for Nordisk Oldkyndighed og Historie 1877. pp. 1–128.

Müller, S., 1888. Ordning af Danmarks oldsager. Librarie Renouard, Copenhagen.

Müller, S., 1909. Bronzealderens begyndelse og ældre udvikling i Danmark, efter de nyeste fund. Aarbøger for Nordisk Oldkyndighed og Historie 1909, pp. 1–119.

Murillo-Barroso, M., Martinón-Torres, M., 2012. Amber sources and trade in the prehistory of the Iberian Peninsula. European Journal of Archaeology 15 (2), 187–216.

Myhre, B., 1980. Sola og Madla i førhistorisk tid. In Myhre, B., Lindanger, B., Tjelta, H. (eds.), Soga om Sola og Madla. Sola kommune, Sola, pp. 11–170.

Myhre, B., 1981. Sola og Madla i førhistorisk tid. Museum of Archaeology Stavanger, Stavanger.

Myhre, L. N., 1998. Historier fra en annen virkelighet: Fortellinger om bronsealderen ved Karmsundet. Museum of Archaeology Stavanger, Stavanger.

Myhre, L. N., 2004. Trialectic archaeology: Monuments and space in Southwest Norway 1700–500 BC. Museum of Archaeology Stavanger, Stavanger.

Needham, S. P., 2009. Encompassing the sea: "Maritories" and Bronze Age maritime interaction. In Clark, P. (ed.), Bronze Age connections: Cultural contact in prehistoric Europe. Oxbow Books, Oxford, pp. 12–37.

Nesje, A., Pilø, L. H., Finstad, E., et al., 2012. The climatic significance of artefacts related to prehistoric reindeer hunting exposed at melting ice patches in southern Norway. The Holocene 22 (4), 485–496.

Nilsson, A., 2011. Making a simple tool: Bronze casting for personal use in the latter part of the Scandinavian Bronze Age. Lund Archaeological Review 17, 85–90.

Nimura, C., Skoglund, P., Bradley, R., 2020. Navigating inland: Bronze Age watercraft and the lakes of Southern Sweden. European Journal of Archaeology 23 (2), 186–206.

Nørgaard, H. W., Pernicka, E., Vandkilde, H., 2019. On the trail of Scandinavia's early metallurgy: Provenance, transfer and mixing. PloS One 14 (7), e0219574.

Nyegaard, G., 2018. Bronze Age animal husbandry: The faunal remains from Bjerre Enge. In Bech, J.- H., Eriksen, B. V., Kristiansen, K. (eds.), Bronze age settlement and land-use in Thy, northwest Denmark. Museum Thy & Jutland Archaeological Society, Højbjerg & Thisted, pp. 469–476.

O'Brien, W., 2015. Prehistoric copper mining in Europe: 5500–500 BC. Oxford University Press, Oxford.

Odriozola, C. P., Sousa, A. C., Mataloto, R., et al., 2019. Amber, beads and social interaction in the Late Prehistory of the Iberian Peninsula: An update. Archaeological and Anthropological Sciences 11 (2), 567–595.

Olausson, D., 1988. Dots on a map: Thoughts about the way archaeologists study prehistoric trade and exchange. Acta Archaeologica Lundensia 8 (16), 15–24.

Olsen, A. B., 2009. Transition to farming in Western Norway seen as a rapid replacement of landscapes. In McCartan, S. (ed.), Mesolithic horizons. Papers presented at the seventh International Conference on the Mesolithic in Europe, Belfast 2005. Oxbow, Oxford, pp. 589–596.

Olsen, A. B., 2013. Jordbrukskulturens pionertid på Vestlandet: Hus, åker og territorialitet. In Diinhoff, S., Ramstad, M., Slinning, T. (eds.), Jordbruksbosetningens utvikling på Vestlandet. Seminar om dagens kunnskapsstatus, presentasjon av nye resultater og fremtidige problemstillinger. Universitetet i Bergen, Bergen, pp. 129–148.

Olsen, A.-L. H., Earle, T. K., 2018. Bjerre 6. In Bech, J.-H., Eriksen, B. V., Kristiansen, K. (eds.), Bronze age settlement and land-use in Thy, northwest Denmark. Museum Thy & Jutland Archaeological Society, Højbjerg & Thisted, pp. 89–109.

Oma, K. A., 2018. The sheep people: The ontology of making lives, building homes and forging herds in Early Bronze Age Norway. Equinox, Sheffield.

Oma, K.A., 2020. Contrasting the Women in the Rege and Molkhaug Mounds: Poised Between the Here and the Beyond. Contrasts of the Nordic Bronze Age, vol. 1 The Archaeology of Northern Europe. Brepols, Turnhout, pp. 259–268.

Oma, K. A., 2020. On the Fringe: Sheepdogs and their status within Bronze Age Ontologies in Scandinavia. Current Swedish Archaeology 28, 99–120.

Østmo, E., 2008. Some notes on the development of shipbuilding and overseas connections in Scandinavian prehistory. In Lund, J., Prescott, C., Chilidis, K. (eds.), Facets of archeology. Essays in Honour of Lotte Hedeager on Her 60th Birthday. University of Oslo, Oslo, pp. 265–274.

Pernicka, E., 2010. Archäometallurgische Untersuchungen am und zum Hortfund von Nebra. In Meller, H., Bertemes, F. (eds.), Der Griff nach den Sternen. Wie Europas Eliten zu Macht und Reichtum kamen. Beier & Beran, Langenweißbach, pp. 719–734.

Pernicka, E., Lutz, J., Stöllner, T., 2016. Bronze Age copper produced at Mitterberg, Austria, and its distribution. Archaeologia Austriaca 100, 19–56.

Persson, M., Andersson, F., Guinard, M., Lindkvist, A., 2002. Bronsålderslämningar i Kumla: Gravar och gropar. Societas Archaeologica Upsaliensis, Uppsala.

Petersson, H., 2009. Kokgroparna vid Kind. Bohusläns museum, Uddevalla.

Podėnas, V., Čivilytė, A., 2019. Bronze casting and communication in the southeastern Baltic Bronze Age. Lietuvos Archeologija 45, 169–199.

Polanyi, K., 2001. The great transformation: The political and economic origins of our time. Beacon Press, Boston.

Polanyi, K., Arensberg, C. M., Pearson, H. W., 1957. Trade and market in the early empires: Economies in history and theory. Free Press, Glencoe.

Prentiss, A. M., Cross, G., Foor, T. A., et al., 2008. Evolution of a late prehistoric winter village on the interior Plateau of British Columbia: Geophysical investigations, radiocarbon dating, and spatial analysis of the bridge river site. American Antiquity 73 (1), 59–82.

Prescott, C., 1991a. Kulturhistoriske undersøkelser i Skrivarhelleren. Universitetet i Bergen, Bergen.

Prescott, C., 1991b. Late Neolithic and Bronze Age developments on the periphery of Southern Scandinavia. Norwegian Archaeological Review 24 (1), 35–48.

Prescott, C., 1994. Paradigm gained - paradigm lost? 150 years of Norwegian Bronze Age research. Norwegian Archaeological Review 27 (2), 87–109.

Prescott, C., 1995. Aspects of Early Pastoralism in Sogn, Norway. Acta Archaeologica 66, 163–190.

Prescott, C., 1996. Was there really a Neolithic in Norway? Antiquity 70 (267), 77–87.

Prescott, C., 2012. The origin of a Bronze Age in Norway: Structure, regional process and localized history. In Anfinset, N., Wrigglesworth, M. (eds.), Local societies in Bronze Age Northern Europe. Routledge, New York, pp. 215–231.

Prescott, C., Melheim, A. L., 2017. Textiles from the periphery: Upland evidence from Norway. In Bergerbrant, S., Wessman, A. (eds.), New perspectives on the Bronze Age. Proceedings of the 13th Nordic Bronze Age Symposium held in Gothenburg 9th to 13th June 2015. Archaeopress, Oxford, pp. 313–325.

Prescott, C., Sand-Eriksen, A., Austvoll, K. I., 2018. The sea and Bronze Age transformations. In Holt, E. (ed.), Water and power in past societies. State University of New York Press, Albany, pp. 177–198.

Price, N., 2016. Pirates of the North Sea? The Viking ship as a political space. In Glørstad, H., Tsigaridas Glørstad, A. Z., Melheim, L. (eds.), Comparative perspectives on past colonisation, maritime interaction and cultural integration. Equinox, Sheffield, pp. 149–176.

Price, T. D., Frei, R., Brinker, U., et al., 2019. Multi-isotope proveniencing of human remains from a Bronze Age battlefield in the Tollense Valley in northeast Germany. Archaeological and Anthropological Sciences 11 (1), 33–49.

Prøsch-Danielsen, L., 1993. Prehistoric agriculture revealed by pollen analysis, plough-marks and sediment studies at Sola, south-western Norway. Vegetation History and Archaeobotany 2 (4), 233–244.

Prøsch-Danielsen, L., Prescott, C., Fredh, E. D., 2020. Land cover and exploitation of upland resources on the Høg-Jæren Plateau, southwestern Norway, over the last 6500 years. Journal of Archaeological Science 32, 102443.

Prøsch-Danielsen, L., Simonsen, A., 2000. The deforestation patterns and the establishment of the coastal heathland of southwestern Norway. Museum of Archaeology Stavanger, Stavanger.

Prøsch-Danielsen, L., Soltvedt, E.-C., 2011. From saddle to rotary: Hand Querns in South-Western Norway and the corresponding crop plant assemblages. Acta Archaeologica 82, 129–162.

Prøsch-Danielsen, L., Soltvedt, E.-C., 2012. Føstemann til mølla: De ulike kvernsteinstypene og kornsortene som ble malt på dem gjennom forhistorisk tid i Rogaland. Frá haug ok heiðni 3, 50–61.

Pulak, C., 1998. The Uluburun shipwreck: An overview. International Journal of Nautical Archaeology 27 (3), 188–224.

Randsborg, K., 1969. Von Periode II zu III: Chronologische Studien über die ältere Bronzezeit Südskandinavien und Norddeutschlands. Acta Archaeologica 39, 1–142.

Randsborg, K., 1995. Hjortspring: Warfare and sacrifice in early Europe. Aarhus University Press, Aarhus.

Rasmussen, M., 1999. Livestock without bones: The long-house as contributor to the interpretation of livestock management in the Southern Scandinavian Early Bronze Age. In Fabech, C. E., Ringtved, J. E. (eds.), Settlement and landscape. Jutland Archaeological Society, Højbjerg pp. 281–290.

Rassmann, K., 2010. Metallverbrauch in der frühen Bronzezeit Mitteleuropas: Produktion, Zirkulation und Konsumption frühbronzezeitlicher Metallobjekte als Untersuchungsgegenstände einer archäologischen Wirtschaftsgeschichte. Archäologie in Eurasien 24, 341–363.

Regnell, M., Sjögren, K.-G., 2006. Introduction and development of agriculture. In Sjögren, K.-G. (ed.), Ecology and economy in Stone and Bronze Age Scania. Skånska spår: arkeologi längs Västkustbanen. Riksantikvarieämbetet, Stockholm, pp. 106–169.

Renfrew, C., 1974. Beyond a subsistence economy: The evolution of social organisation in prehistoric Europe. In Moore, C. B. (ed.), Reconstructing complex societies. An Archaeological Colloquium. American Schools of Oriental Research, Cambridge, pp. 69–95.

Renfrew, C., 1975. Trade as action at a distance: Questions of integration and communication. In Sabloff, J. A., Lamberg-Karlovsky, C. C. (eds.), Ancient civilization and trade. University of New Mexico Press, Albuquerque, pp. 3–60.

Renfrew, C., 1986. Introduction: Peer polity interaction and socio-political change. In Renfrew, C., Cherry, J. F. (eds.), Peer polity interaction and socio-political change. New Directions in Archaeology. Cambridge University Press, Cambridge, pp. 1–18.

Ricardo, D., 2004. The principles of political economy and taxation. Dover, Mineola.

Rogers, J. S., 2011. Czech logboats: Early inland watercraft from Bohemia and Moravia. Studia Minora Facultatis Philosophicae Universitatis Brunensis 16, 171–202.

Rowlands, M. J., Larsen, M., Kristiansen, K. (eds.), 1987. Centre and periphery in the ancient world. New directions in Archaeology. Cambridge University Press, Cambridge.

Runge, M. T., 2012. Yngre bronzealders bebyggelse indenfor et 350 hektar stort undersøgelsesområde sydøst for Odense. In Boddum, S., Mikkelsen, M., Terkildsen, N. (eds.), Bebyggelsen i yngre bronzealders lokale kulturlandskab. Viborg Museum and Holstebro Museum, Viborg, Holstebro, pp. 113–139.

Sabatini, S., Bergerbrant, S. (eds.), 2020. The textile revolution in Bronze Age Europe: Production, specialisation, consumption. Cambridge University Press, Cambridge.

Sahlins, M. D., 1965. On the sociology of primitive exchange. In Banton, M. (ed.), The relevance of models for social anthropology. Routledge, London, pp. 138–236.

Sahlins, M. D., 1972. Stone age economics. Aldine, Piscataway.

Sherratt, A., 1993. What would a Bronze-Age world system look like? Relations between temperate Europe and the Mediterranean in later prehistory. Journal of European Archaeology 1 (2), 1–58.

Shetelig, H., 1925. Norges forhistorie: Problemer og resultater i norsk arkæologi. Aschehoug, Oslo.

Singer, F., Singer, S.S., 1963. Industrial ceramics. Chapman & Hall, London.

Skoglund, P., 2009. Beyond chiefs and networks: Corporate strategies in Bronze Age Scandinavia. Journal of Social Archaeology 9 (2), 200–219.

Solheim, S., 2021. Timing the emergence and development of arable farming in southeastern Norway using summed probability distribution of radiocarbon dates and a Bayesian Age Model. Radiocarbon 63 (5), 1503–1524.

Soltvedt, E.-C., 2007. Bøndene på Kvålehodlene: Boplass-, jordbruks- og landskapsutvikling gjennom 6000 år på Jæren, SV Norge. AmS-Varia 47. Arkeologisk museum i Stavanger, Stavanger.

Sørensen, L., Karg, S., 2014. The expansion of agrarian societies towards the north: New evidence for agriculture during the Mesolithic/Neolithic transition in Southern Scandinavia. Journal of Archaeological Science 51, 98–114.

Sörman, A., 2017. A place for crafting? Late Bronze Age metalworking in southern Scandinavia and the issue of workshops. In Brysbaert, A., Gorgues, A. (eds.), Artisans versus nobility? Multiple identities of elites and "commoners" viewed through the lens of crafting from the Chalcolithic to the Iron Ages in Europe and the Mediterranean. Sidestone Press, Leiden, pp. 53–78.

Sörman, A., 2018. Gjutningens arenor: Metallhantverkets rumsliga, sociala och politiska organisation i södra Skandinavien under bronsåldern. PhD. University of Stockholm, Stockholm.

Stika, H.-P., Heiss, A. G., 2013. Bronzezeitliche Landwirtschaft in Europa: Der Versuch einer Gesamtdarstellung des Forschungsstandes. In Willroth, K.-H. (ed.), Siedlungen der ältere Bronzezeit. Beiträge zur Siedlungsarchäologie und Paläoökologie des zweiten vorchristlichen Jahrtausends in Südskandinavien, Norddeutschland und den Niederlanden. Wachholtz Verlag, Neumünster, pp. 189–222.

Streiffert, J., 2004. Hus från bronsåldern och äldre järnåldern i Bohuslän. In Claesson, P., Munkenberg, B. (eds.), Landskap och bebyggelse. Bohusläns museum, Uddevalla, pp. 135–154.

Syvertsen, K., 2005. Rogalands ristninger i graver som transformerende og stabiliserende faktorer i tilværelsen. In Goldhahn, J. (ed.), Mellan sten och järn. Intellecta, Göteborg, pp. 503–520.

Thrane, H., 1998. The effects of the Bronze Age on the environment and culture in Scandinavia. In Hänsel, B. (ed.), Mensch und Umvelt in der Bronzezeit Europas. Oetker-Voges, Kiel, pp. 271–280.

Thrane, H., 2013. Scandinavia. In Fokkens, H., Harding, A. F. (eds.), The Oxford handbook of the European Bronze Age. Oxford University Press, Oxford, pp. 1–23.

Trigger, B. G., 2006. A history of archaeological thought. Cambridge University Press, Cambridge.

Ullén, I. (ed.), 2003. Arkeologi på Väg: Undersökningar för E18. Bronsåldersboplatsen vid Apalle i Uppland: Uppland, Övergrans Socken, Apalle. Swedish National Heritage Board, Stockholm.

Valbjørn, K. V., 2003. A hypothetical "Hjortspring skinboat." In Crumlin-Pedersen, O., Trakadas, A. (eds.), Hjortspring. A Pre-Roman Iron-Age warship in context. Viking Ship Museum, Roskilde, pp. 137–140.

Vandkilde, H., 1996. From stone to bronze: The metalwork of the late Neolithic and earliest Bronze Age in Denmark. Aarhus University Press, Aarhus.

Vandkilde, H., 2007. Culture and change in Central European prehistory: 6th to 1st millennium BC. Aarhus University Press, Aarhus.

Vandkilde, H., 2014. Breakthrough of the Nordic Bronze Age: Transcultural warriorhood and a Carpathian crossroad in the sixteenth century BC. European Journal of Archaeology 17 (4), 602–633.

Vandkilde, H., 2016. Bronzization: The Bronze Age as pre-modern globalization. Praehistorische Zeitschrift 91 (1), 103–123.

Vandkilde, H., Matta, V., Ahlqvist, L., Nørgaard, H. W., 2022. Anthropomorphised warlike beings with horned helmets: Bronze Age Scandinavia, Sardinia, and Iberia compared. Praehistorische Zeitschrift 97 (1), 130–158.

Varberg, J., 2005. Flint og metal: Mellan stenalder og bronzealder i Sydskandinavien. In Goldhahn, J. (ed.), Mellan sten och järn, vol. 1. Intellecta, Göteborg, pp. 67–79.

Varberg, J., Gratuze, B., Kaul, F., 2015. Between Egypt, Mesopotamia and Scandinavia: Late Bronze Age glass beads found in Denmark. Journal of Archaeological Science 54, 168–181.

Varberg, J., Gratuze, B., Kaul, F., et al., 2016. Mesopotamian glass from Late Bronze Age Egypt, Romania, Germany, and Denmark. Journal of Archaeological Science 74, 184–194.

Vinner, M., 2003. Sea trials. In Crumlin-Pedersen, O., Trakadas, A. (eds.), Hjortspring. A pre-roman iron- age warship in context. Viking Ship Museum, Roskilde, pp. 103–118.

von Arbin, S., Lindberg, M., 2017. News on the Byslätt Bark "Canoe." In Litwin, J., Kentley, E. (eds.), Baltic and beyond. Change and continuity in shipbuilding : Proceedings of the Fourteenth International Symposium on Boat and Ship Archaeology Gdańsk 2015. National Maritime Museum, Gdańsk, pp. 245–250.

Wallerstein, I., 1974. The rise and future demise of the world capitalist system: Concepts for comparative analysis. Comparative Studies in Society and History 16 (4), 387–415.

Wallerstein, I. 2011. Capitalist agriculture and the origins of the European world-economy in the sixteenth century. University of California Press, Berkley.

Wang, Q., Strekopytov, S., Roberts, B. W., 2018. Copper ingots from a probable Bronze Age shipwreck off the coast of Salcombe, Devon: Composition and microstructure. Journal of Archaeological Science 97, 102–117.

Wang, Q., Strekopytov, S., Roberts, B. W., Wilkin, N., 2016. Tin ingots from a probable Bronze Age shipwreck off the coast of Salcombe, Devon: Composition and microstructure. Journal of Archaeological Science 67, 80–92.

Watkins, T., 1980. A prehistoric coracle in Fife. International Journal of Nautical Archaeology and Underwater Exploration 9 (4), 277–286.

Wehlin, J., 2013. Östersjöns skeppssättningar: Monument och mötesplatser under yngre bronsålder. PhD. University of Gothenburg, Gothenburg.

Williams, R. A., Le Carlier de Veslud, C., 2019. Boom and bust in Bronze Age Britain: Major copper production from the Great Orme mine and European trade, c . 1600–1400 BC. Antiquity 93 (371), 1178–1196.

Woltermann, G., 2016. Amber before metal: Die frühbronzezeitliche Bernsteinschmucksitte Norddeutschlands zwischen lokalem Kontext und transeuropäischen Fernkontakten. In Jockenhövel, A. (ed.), 50 Jahre "Prähistorische Bronzefunde." Bilanz und Perspektiven: Beiträge zum internationalen Kolloquium vom 24. bis 26. September 2014 in Mainz. Prähistorische Bronzefunde XX, 14. Franz Steiner Verlag, Stuttgart, pp. 383–409.

Wright, E. V., 2016. The Ferriby boats: Seacraft of the Bronze Age. Routledge, London.

Zilmer, K., 2006. The representation of waterborne traffic in old norse narratives: The case of the Baltic Sea area. Viking and Medieval Scandinavia 2 (1), 239–274.

Acknowledgments

The work on this volume was funded by the Swedish Research Council (2020–01097) and Riksbankens Jubileumsfond (M21-0018). We are grateful to the three editors Timothy Keese Earle, Emily Jean Kate, and Kenneth Gale Hirth for inviting us to write this volume and for their help bringing this volume to publication. Furthermore, we thank the three anonymous peer reviewers for their feedback which helped to improve this volume. Ashely Green and Rich Potter deserve our gratitude for their help with illustrations and the Swedish Rock Art Research Archives for providing rock art documentation. Lastly, we are very indebted to Mikael Fauvelle for helping us with constructive comments and language editing. All remaining errors are our own.

Cambridge Elements

Elements in Ancient and Premodern Economies

Kenneth G. Hirth

The Pennsylvania State University

Ken Hirth's research focuses on the development of ranked and state-level societies in the New World. He is interested in political economy and how forms of resource control lead to the development of structural inequalities. Topics of special interest include: exchange systems, craft production, settlement patterns, and preindustrial urbanism. Methodological interests include: lithic technology and use-wear, ceramics, and spatial analysis.

Timothy Earle

Northwestern University

Tim Earle is an economic anthropologist specializing in the archaeological studies of social inequality, leadership, and political economy in early chiefdoms and states. He has conducted field projects in Polynesia, Peru, Argentina, Denmark, and Hungary. Having studied the emergence of social complexity in three world regions, his work is comparative, searching for the causes of alternative pathways to centralized power.

Emily J. Kate

The University of Vienna

Emily Kate is bioarchaeologist with training in radiocarbon dating, isotopic studies, human osteology, and paleodemography. Having worked with projects from Latin America and Europe, her interests include the manner in which paleodietary trends can be used to assess shifts in social and political structure, the affect of migration on societies, and the refinement of regional chronologies through radiocarbon programs.

About the Series

Elements in Ancient and Premodern Economies is committed to critical scholarship on the comparative economies of traditional societies. Volumes either focus on case studies of well documented societies, providing information on domestic and institutional economies, or provide comparative analyses of topical issues related to economic function. Each Element adopts an innovative and interdisciplinary view of culture and economy, offering authoritative discussions of how societies survived and thrived throughout human history.

Cambridge Elements ☰

Elements in Ancient and Premodern Economies